WHAT YOUR PLANNING PROFESSORS FORGOT TO TELL YOU

117 LESSONS EVERY PLANNER SHOULD KNOW

Paul C. Zucker, AICP

PLANNERS PRESS
AMERICAN PLANNING ASSOCIATION
Chicago, Illinois
Washington, D.C.

ILLUSTRATION CREDITS

Chapter 1. Architecture Hall: courtesy University of Nebraska

Chapter 6. Philadelphia City Hall: courtesy Office of the City Representative, Philadelphia; 1962 Bucks County Courthouse: courtesy Bucks County Planning Commission; 1877 Bucks County Courthouse: courtesy Bucks County Planning Commission.

Chapter 12. Coffee hour drawing: Joe Kourakis; Vigeland Park drawing: Joe Kourakis.

Chapter 17. Photo of John T. Howard: courtesy of the Howard family.

Chapter 21. Photo Brookline Town Hall: Jim Walker.

Chapter 24. Photo of Brookline fire station: Jim Walker.

Chapter 38. *Pacific Sun* cover: courtesy Steve McNamara, publisher.

Chapter 40. Photo of Doug Maloney: courtesy Doug Maloney

Chapter 45. Marin County Civic Center: courtesy Marin County.

Chapter 70. Illustrations courtesy Casual Creations, Inc., Huron, California.

Chapter 92. Newspaper article reprinted with permission from the *San Diego Union-Tribune.*

Chapter 102. Newspaper article reprinted with permission from the *San Diego Union-Tribune.*

Chapter 104. Newspaper article by Jack Jones.

Copyright 1999 by the American Planning Association
122 S. Michigan Ave., Suite 1600, Chicago, IL 60603
Paperback edition 1-884829-29-5
Hardbound edition 1-884829-30-9
Library of Congress Catalog Card Number 99-72723

Printed in the United States of America

DEDICATION

To my wife Kathy and sons Erik, Peter, and Andy who both tolerated and supported me during the many tumultuous and crazy times described in this book. My hope is that these experiences enhanced and enriched your lives rather than detracting from your own stories.

I love you all.

CONTENTS

PART 10 CONSULTING..187

ix

ACKNOWLEDGEMENTS

Special thanks to a number of people who reviewed drafts of this book or helped keep my memory of events in touch with what really happened. These include:

Margaret Azevedo, former Marin County Planning Commissioner, one of the smartest and politically astute planning commissioners I've known; **Richard A. Cylinder,** fellow planner in Bucks County who taught me much about planning; **Werner Von Gundell,** my Marin County Deputy Director who was part of the progressive Marin County planning experience; **Lane Kendig,** former Bucks County Planning Commission staff member who shares many fond memories of **Frank Wood; Al Lewis,** a lifelong friend, Berkeley classmate, and another Bucks County alumnus who always has an idea to share; **Bruce McClendon,** Orange County, Florida, Planning Director, another maverick planner who shares my interest in the customer; **Robert E. Moore,** Executive Director, Bucks County Planning Commission, who shared his memories of **Frank Wood; Rick Morey,** my Executive Assistant in San Diego County, who is my mentor and friend; **Roy Potter,** former Fremont, California, Planning Director, who inspired our student planning class at Berkeley; **Jack Siry,** Tucson Assistant Planning Director, a friend and Tucson supporter; **Lydia Stacy,** a secretary who typed much of the draft, laughed at some of my stories, and told me others weren't funny; **Don Vial,** a friend who helped salvage my career after Marin County; **Carol C. Williams,** Assistant Planning Director, Marin County, for research.

Thanks also to **John Woodward,** Brookline, Massachusetts, Planning Director, who helped research my Brookline stories.

Finally, special thanks to **Mike Dukakis,** who taught me so much about government in my early years and so graciously wrote the foreword, and to **Eric Kelly,** an admired APA President, who wrote the introduction.

Credits to **Denise Carabet,** Editing; **Joe Bucknall,** Cover Design and Drawings, Chapters 3, 4, 15, 19, 32, 50, 68, 112; **Dena Cohen,** Typing; **Charles Eaton,** Page Layouts.

FOREWORD

It has been nearly four decades since I first met Paul Zucker when Jack Howard hired him to be the resident planner in Brookline, Massachusetts. A lot of water has flowed over the dam for both of us in the ensuing years.

He spent several years working to help us cope with the pressures and challenges of an older suburb that bordered the city of Boston and was fighting hard to preserve its reputation for good living and good schools. I was an up and coming young politician who had plunged into the political life of his community after returning from military service in Korea and had already run successfully for my first local office while still in law school.

Paul was our second resident planner. His predecessor, Justin Gray, had taught me my first lessons about how a community goes about the business of trying to stay healthy and affordable. Paul picked up where Justin left off, and we worked together on a whole host of issues during the time that he was with us. Fortunately, he decided to try his hand at elective office in Marin County, California, not Brookline, Massachusetts. Otherwise, my political career might have been over before it began.

The 1950s and '60s found most urban communities struggling with the post–World War II surge of suburban growth and urban deterioration, and metropolitan Boston was no exception. Our capital city began experiencing all of the symptoms of urban decline that were infecting older, industrial cities across the nation. State transportation planners were literally paving the way for disinvestment in central cities by building expressways and freeways that not only failed to solve our transportation problems but literally invited businesses and developers to build in the suburbs.

Lovely, historic buildings and precious urban parks were leveled to accommodate the automobile. Public transportation systems like Boston's, which included the oldest subway in America, were permitted to deteriorate, and we were told by the highway engineers that unless we covered cities like Boston and its neighboring suburbs like Brookline with eight-lane expressways and parking garages, we could never compete with the newer suburbs and their shopping malls.

It was people like Paul who helped me to understand just how wrong that advice was and how a great, old city like Boston and its Brookline neighbor could survive and prosper. Sadly, I lost my first major battle on the subject. I led the fight to preserve that wonderful old town hall of ours from the wrecker's ball and its dull and sterile replacement (see Chapter 21), but I lost that battle by a handful of votes in the Brookline town meeting.

I learned a lot of lessons from that experience, and I was one of a handful of young legislators who took on the highway builders and their allies; stopped the so-called Master Highway Plan for metropolitan Boston, which would have put an eight-lane elevated expressway through Boston's famed Emerald Necklace and one of Brookline's loveliest parks; took that highway money and poured it into what is now one of the best transit systems in the country; and helped transform

Boston into one of the nation's—and the world's—great cities.

The rest, as they say, is history. I went on to the governor's office for 12 years and a failed campaign for the presidency. Paul's experiences as a planner, one-time political candidate, nonprofit developer, and management consultant have given him an invaluable fund of knowledge, experience, and wisdom, which he shares with us in this book—a book that should be must reading for planners, politicians, and would-be planners and politicians.

Unfortunately, the problems with which he and I were wrestling in the '60s are still with us, only more so. In fact, urban sprawl has now become a national issue. Some cities and metropolitan areas have learned their lesson, but too many of them are making all the mistakes, and then some, that too many of us were making 35 years ago.

The results are perfectly predictable: declining centers and sprawling suburbs; expressways that are moving parking lots at three in the afternoon; congested airports that drive travelers nuts; and neglected or nonexistent public transit systems.

State governments still don't understand that it is state policies that in too many cases are the culprits. Very few states have coherent growth policies that guide infrastructure investments, the location of major state facilities, state environmental decisions, and state financial assistance to local governments. Regional planning can help, but it is state governments that can really make the difference as we head for a new century.

I loved this book for two reasons.

First, it brought back some very special memories from Paul's and my youth.

Secondly, it gives us the kind of food for thought we need as we work to plan and build communities of the future that provide real economic opportunity for all of their citizens and the kind of quality of life that Americans need and deserve.

Michael S. Dukakis
Boston, Massachusetts
April 1999

INTRODUCTION

Paul Zucker has earned a reputation as one of the leading consultants on management of the planning process. In this book, he shares some of the lessons from more than 40 years of helping communities to make planning work better.

I would, of course, quibble with the title a little. I doubt that Paul's professors "forgot" to tell him these things. Some probably had not learned these lessons because they had spent little or no time in practice, and others undoubtedly placed their priorities on teaching principles of demographic analysis, design, and community development. These 117 lessons come from practice. As both a planning professor and a planning practitioner, I recognize the value of learning from practice. Donald Schoen of the Massachusetts Institute of Technology wrote about the "reflective practitioner." Paul Zucker has done all of that, but he has gone one step further—he has put down these key lessons from his professional life in a lively and highly accessible style. As a professor, I would prefer a title like "117 lessons to study during your first year in practice," although I recognize that it would not sell as well.

The substance of Paul Zucker's work—and his message in this book—is essential to planning practice. His work leaps from the theory of the classroom or studio to the reality of practice in a political world. Part of his message builds on messages taught in traditional planning theory courses: the importance of politics (with a small "p") and participation in the process of developing a plan. Many of his lessons are wonderful examples of "how to make participation work," examples that ought to be taught together with some of the excellent theoretical literature on planning in a democratic society. That part of this book joins Bruce McClendon's excellent work on the subject as learning resources on inclusive planning processes.

The other part of Paul Zucker's message, however, focuses on the core of his work later in his career. Recent graduates of planning programs often believe that a planner or planning agency simply needs to launch a plan with great fanfare and watch it sail to success, as everyone in the community (presumably) recognizes the wisdom of the plan and begins to follow it. Actually, many great plans sink of their own weight, sometimes within weeks after launch. As a planning lawyer, I have long focused on the next step: zoning, capital improvement programs, growth management systems, sign ordinances, and other implementation tools for plans. Such tools take a plan one step closer to effectiveness, but those tools are useful only if handled by effective professionals working in a well-structured, well-managed environment. It is at that point that Paul Zucker's work on management of the planning agency is so important.

Plan implementation requires constant monitoring and careful management of the planning function, both as the plan is prepared and as it is implemented. Planning is a process in more ways than one. He has left that mark directly on several planning agencies that he has managed, but he has affected far more than those. Many other agencies have learned from his recommendations to them as a consultant, and hundreds of planning managers have taken home his ideas from his popular workshops. In this book, we have the opportunity to learn Paul Zucker's trade secrets—and, for those of us who have learned from them already, we have a lively and handy refresher course. It is one that I will use as a formal learning resource in the "professional practice" course that I teach, and one that I recommend highly to others for both structured study and individual study.

Eric Damian Kelly, FAICP
Muncie, Indiana
April 1999

PREFACE

I first started thinking about the stories in this book during the many hours I spent on airplanes and in airports during a busy consulting year in 1998. I thought it would be fun to write them down for my own amusement. So each flight I scribbled off a story or two in longhand—no notes—just fond memories. Gradually it dawned on me that the stories and the resulting lessons were a large part of my planning learning. They not only educated me, but also, perhaps, could help others.

This is not intended to be an autobiography, but it is a journey. A journey through the ups and downs of a planning career that spanned many states, cities, counties, consulting, and nonprofits. A journey from the East Coast to the West Coast, with spaces in between and still unfolding.

Once I had a draft, I searched my files to confirm my memory, sent various chapters to others who had shared the same experiences and was delighted to discover that the stories were all true—for better or worse.

I hope you enjoy reading them as much as I did living them.

Paul C. Zucker
March 1999

P.S. I'd love to hear some of your stories. E-mail them to me, **paul@zuckersystems.com.** If you like we'll share them with others via our web page:
www.zuckersystems.com

PART 1

NEBRASKA

1

WHY NOT BE AN ARCHITECT?
OR A FRUSTRATED PLANNER?

My journey toward city planning started in 1952 when I enrolled in the University of Nebraska's (Go Big Red! 1970, 1971, 1994, 1995 and 1997 National Football Champion Cornhuskers) Architecture program. Not a particularly well known program, my class had only 10 students. It was housed in a somewhat decrepit old building (since declared historic) which had its 15 minutes of fame when it was later used for the filming of "Terms of Endearment."

University of Nebraska, Architecture Hall

I thought that I was naturally led to architecture having had a workshop in our basement, having helped my brother build a house, and having produced quilting frames for all my mother's friends.

Talk about a rude awakening. In the course of launching my architecture career I discovered:

- I had to draw. I can't.

- I had to learn calculus—twice.

- I would struggle two months on a design whereas one of my classmates would saunter in two days before the project was due and draw awesome designs much better than mine.

- One of my house designs, cleverly done in orange and green, was used for years after I left as a multifaceted example of how not to do it.

- One of my classmates always beat me to the punch by cornering the latest architectural magazine whose latest fad would then magically appear on his drafting table. He later became dean of a prestigious architectural school.

- The best architectural job offer I received upon graduation was in cool Duluth, Minnesota (that's cold, not cool).

I was also offered a job as a planner, sight unseen, by either them or me, for Bucks County, Pennsylvania. I went to see my Dean, Lynus Burr Smith (what a great name for an architect). His advice was straightforward and simple: "If you want to spend the rest of your life frustrated, become a city planner." I did. But rather than being frustrated, I've experienced a delightful 40 years.

LESSON 1

If you can't draw, become a city planner. It may be frustrating, but it can also be rewarding and challenging.

2
DECISIONS

Several days before my Nebraska graduation, I married a beautiful Norwegian girl from Minnesota. Since I hadn't yet finished my thesis, designing a concert hall, we spent our honeymoon in a rented apartment where I stayed up until three or four in the morning, drawing. My concert hall had a delicate tile pattern on all the floors and my instructor demanded that I draw every floor tile on 30-by-40-inch boards using a special tea for ink—and some think city planning can be tedious. Generally, when I finally straggled to bed, my new wife would sit up and ask me who I was and what I was doing there.

In spite of my dean's admonition, my decision to become a city planner was quite easy. I had two job offers, one as a planner in Bucks County, the other as an architect in Duluth, Minnesota. Neither my wife nor I had spent much time out of the Midwest, and the thought of living on the East Coast in Bucks County was intriguing. Also, my wife grew up in Minnesota and was well acquainted with the weather in Duluth.

As an architectural student I found that if we were given a totally unconstrained, flat site, we had trouble coming up with a design. However, given a tight site, steep slopes, trees, stream, or other constraints, design came easily. The same lessons operate in city planning and in selecting a job.

LESSON 2
Decisions are easy when you have few choices.

On our way East to become a planner.

PART 2

BUCKS COUNTY

Learning to be a Planner

3
WHAT PLANNERS DO—
OR DON'T!

Bucks County was a good choice for a young architect who knew little about planning. Ed Bacon was
plying his trade next door in Philadelphia. Bucks
County's Planning Director, Franklin Wood, under-
stood the politics of planning better than anyone I've
met since, and he threw great parties!

My first assignment came from a planner I was replacing, another architect. The department was working
on a new freeway location and I was to draw a perspective of the freeway and a freeway interchange. I
had driven 1,500 miles pulling a U-Haul for this
assignment?

LESSON 3
Drawing perspectives of freeway interchanges
isn't city planning.

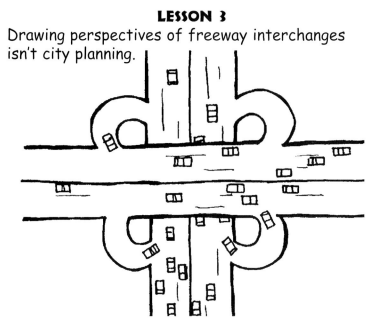

4
DO SOMETHING

Early on, it became clear that although the office was good at politics, no one had a clear picture of what planning was. Only one staffer even had a planning degree and he spent most of his time on administration. I was left to flounder on my own.

Not knowing what else to do, I jumped in:

> • I read all the old reports and organized them into a bibliography and library.

> • I learned how to battle with the Pennsylvania Department of Highways over freeway locations and frontage road designs.

> • I created a manual Geographic Information System (GIS). We discovered that if you could put separate data on clear Mylar, you could combine various data by stacking maps and making prints in a large vacuum machine. Our maps were three-feet-by-six-feet in size and unwieldy. In this roundabout way, I became known as the mapmaking king; an effort described in an unpublished history[†] of Bucks County planning as follows:

"In the middle 1950s, Mylar, a much stronger and dimensionally stable material became generally available. Land Planner Paul C. Zucker, a recent architectural graduate of the University of Nebraska, converted much of the information assembled over the five years of the Planning Commission's existence to Mylar sheets. Using color-separated one inch to 2,000 feet U.S.G.S. information as the base, he showed the entire county on five overlapping map sheets. He then produced a wide array of additional infor-

---

[†]Unpublished draft by Richard A. Cylinder, 1988.

mation on separate overlays including individual land use categories, stream valleys, drainage areas, steep slopes, water and sewer mains and service areas, census data, historical development patterns, highway and land use proposals, traffic data, zoning districts, etc. Although Mylar was expensive, it was extremely durable and allowed production of cheap prints in any combination of overlays."

• I became so enamored with maps that the staff wrote a song, "Paul's Lament," about it to the tune of "Wouldn't It Be Loverly."

All I want is a map somewhere
　With a Zip-a-Tone here and some Leroy there.
　And a legend lined up square
　Oh, wouldn't it be loverly?

Lots of Mylar for me to use,
　Lots of red tapes and lots of blues,
And a draftsman I won't lose
Oh, wouldn't it be loverly?

Someone find me another drawer
For all my maps I need more and more
　They're piling on the floor
　Ten drawers would be so loverly.

LESSON 4
　When you don't know what to do, just do something.

5
CROSSROAD TOWNS

Kathy and I moved to a century-old carriage house owned by and next door to an original exurbanite—a New York doctor who commuted 180 miles per day to live in the splendor of Bucks County in a classic 1800s stone farm house. The farm house was located in the middle of 80 acres. In the evening the doctor, coming home, would walk past our living room window in his three piece suit. A few minutes later he was walking the other way dressed in overalls and ready to be a Bucks County farmer. Our carriage house was two miles from Wycomb, Pennsylvania, a crossroads town with one gas station and a handful of houses.

1800s Farm House and Carriage House

Wycomb got me thinking about the other 100 or so crossroad towns in Bucks County and how they might form a focus for planning. As part of my "do something" approach to planning, I completed a study documenting all the towns. These burgs had quaint names like Carversville, Chalfont, Gardensville, Fallsington, Lumberville, Mechanicsville, Point Pleasant, Riegelsville, Rushland, Soudertown, and Sellersville. We weren't smart enough to figure out how to use this study, but in hindsight I believe it could have become the framework for much of Bucks County's planning.

LESSON 5
Crossroad towns and historic settlements can be used as a basis for structuring a plan.

6
PHILADELPHIA CITY HALL

A nother assignment I had in Bucks County was working on the layout for the planning office to be located in a new (1962) County Courthouse, replacing the old 1877 County Courthouse. The office layout worked, but can you imagine replacing this...

...with this?

Bucks County Courthouse, 1877

Bucks County Courthouse, 1962

The economics of replacing the old county court-house undoubtedly made sense, but I'm reminded of the study written in 1957 whether to rehabilitate or demolish the venerable 1874 Philadelphia City Hall. The best part of the consultant's analysis and the winning proposition was simply this: What would Philadelphia be like without it?

Philadelphia City Hall

LESSON 6
When replacing historic structures, the new is almost always worse than the old.

7
SPRAWL

Having given the impression that I knew what I was doing, I soon was placed in charge of creating Bucks County's first ever countywide plan. I was a bit overwhelmed, but was assigned a newly hired assistant who had both a planning degree and a creative mind. Attilio A. Bergamasco—with a name like that, he was bound to be creative. One of Archie's first thoughts was that sprawl, in and of itself, is not all bad. In fact, he suggested sprawl provides options to round out the community later with things either we or the developer forgot to plan for or build.

We memorialized Archie's concept in one of our countywide principles as follows: *"Any plan or program must not only sense the needs of the present and the predictable future, but must, within the limitations of cost and feasibility, be capable of adapting easily and effectively to unforeseen or uncertain changes in technology, the economy or social customs."*

This lesson was reinforced by another event in 1959. One of the large Levittowns was built in Bucks County. Somewhat to the north of this was a smaller development, called Fairless Hills. The vacant land in between these developments was owned by U.S. Steel and was surrounded by the two developments. It was like a hole in a doughnut. We saw that site as an opportunity to create a focus for the two sprawling, nondescript single-family areas by building a new city core. We kicked this idea around in the office, but it hadn't gone very far.

One day, Franklin Wood, the planning director, with his extensive contacts and political skills, walked in the office and announced he'd arranged to meet representatives of U.S. Steel to present our ideas—the next day. That day Frank drove while another planner, Dick Cylinder, and I sat in the back seat frantically applying zipatone and other finishing touches to the drawings as we drove to the meeting.

The meeting did not begin auspiciously. When I began my presentation, the U.S. Steel representative interrupted and unrolled his own plans for the hole in the doughnut, which consisted of more nondescript development. He showed no interest in our plan. Nevertheless, we left the meeting with the idea that we would continue to pursue the plan. I left Bucks County in 1961, and I'm told that after I left the idea was presented to the three municipalities that bisected the area. They were all enthusiastic but fought over who would get the taxable goodies, and the concept lost its steam. Today, the area is a mishmash of this and that. What a lost opportunity.

LESSON 7
Sprawl is not all bad; plan for unforeseen circumstances.

8
THE GENERAL PLAN BELONGS ON A CAKE

Although I wasn't there to finish it, Bucks County's General Plan was completed shortly before the 1962 national APA conference that was held in Atlantic City.

Franklin Wood's communication and social skills once again rose to the occasion. As a young planner I was always impressed by Frank. He was one of those people who could enter an elevator, and by the time he got to his floor, he knew everyone on the elevator and may have been invited to the next party. Somewhere in Franklin's travels he met the queen of an unremarkable country (I can't remember where) who happened to own a marvelous Art Deco house on the Atlantic City boardwalk that she seldom used. Franklin was told if he ever needed a place to stay in Atlantic City to be her guest. So, for the conference, it became the Bucks County Planning Department headquarters. To celebrate the completion of the General Plan, Franklin had a large cake prepared that displayed the plan, in some detail, in the frosting.[†] As a former staff member, I was asked to help tend bar for the party. It seemed like we entertained more people at this party than APA had at its conference. Among my memories was pouring premixed martinis out of three-gallon water bottles.

[†]In conducting research for this book I was told that my replacement in Bucks County, Archie Bergamasco, baked and decorated the cake. He and another planner had left the county to start a consulting practice. They also opened a restaurant over an old A&P grocery store. Archie became known as a long-range planner and short order cook.

Franklin Wood passed away in 1997. The alumni in that great Bucks County planning program have dozens of interesting stories about Franklin's politics and parties. If you want to know more, call Lane Kendig, the guru of performance zoning, at 847-949-8288; Professor Al Lewis at 315-470-6539; or Dick Cylinder at 215-493-5267.

LESSON 8

Make connections in the elevator. You never know when you may need them.

While I was in Bucks County, Franklin Wood bought an old stone farm house and we would periodically help with repairs. This photo taken in front of that house shows left to right: unknown; Franklin Wood; Frank's sister, Sally; Bill Davis, one of the few members on the staff with a planning degree; unknown; Paul Zucker.

9
FIND OUT WHAT YOU'RE DOING

Although I was moving ahead by appearing to know what I was doing, it soon occurred to me that maybe I should find out what planning was really all about. I had taken a few planning classes with the Philadelphia Planning Director, Ed Bacon, at the Wharton School in Philadelphia, and my switch from architecture to city planning was looking better and better.

The list of prospective planning schools was much shorter then than it is today, with Harvard, MIT, Penn, North Carolina, Berkeley the best choices. I liked MIT but wasn't accepted. During those years, each major planning school could give one large grant each year to a new student. The grants were from the Sears Foundation and the students were called Sears Fellows. The program was later discontinued, but was great for the planning profession while it lasted.

When I was offered a $5,000 cash, no-strings-attached Sears Fellowship to Berkeley, my decision became easy: Follow the money.

The money not only allowed my wife and me to spend seven weeks in Europe between my first and second year at Berkeley, but also to buy and bring back a new Volkswagen convertible. What a way to go to school!

Ten years or so after the Sears Foundation program was discontinued, the foundation had a reception at a national APA conference for all former fellows. Before the foundation speaker took the podium, several of us cooked up a scheme to suggest that Sears sponsor *former* Sears Fellows on creative research sabbaticals. I'm sorry to say that the free booze and carrot sticks were the only contribution the foundation made to this idea.

LESSON 9

Follow the money.

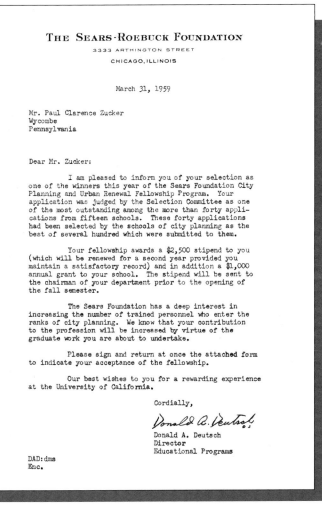

THE SEARS-ROEBUCK FOUNDATION

3333 ARTHINGTON STREET

CHICAGO, ILLINOIS

March 31, 1959

Mr. Paul Clarence Zucker
Wycombe
Pennsylvania

Dear Mr. Zucker:

    I am pleased to inform you of your selection as one of the winners this year of the Sears Foundation City Planning and Urban Renewal Fellowship Program. Your application was judged by the Selection Committee as one of the most outstanding among the more than forty applications from fifteen schools. These forty applications had been selected by the schools of city planning as the best of several hundred which were submitted to them.

    Your fellowship awards a $2,500 stipend to you (which will be renewed for a second year provided you maintain a satisfactory record) and in addition a $1,000 annual grant to your school. The stipend will be sent to the chairman of your department prior to the opening of the fall semester.

    The Sears Foundation has a deep interest in increasing the number of trained personnel who enter the ranks of city planning. We know that your contribution to the profession will be increased by virtue of the graduate work you are about to undertake.

    Please sign and return at once the attached form to indicate your acceptance of the fellowship.

    Our best wishes to you for a rewarding experience at the University of California.

Cordially,

Donald A. Deutsch

Donald A. Deutsch
Director
Educational Programs

DAD:dms
Enc.

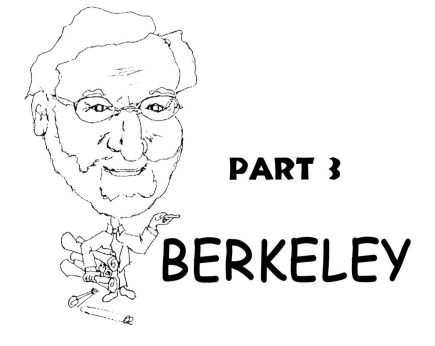

PART 3

BERKELEY

10
WHAT PLANNERS DO REVISITED—THE BERKELEY DAZE

I went back to school to find out what it is that planners do. Some faculty and students led by Jack Kent[†] felt the focus should be on physical planning. Other faculty members, such as Melvin M. Webber, J.W. (Jack) Dyckman, and Barclay Gibbs Jones, were pushing the field into social/economic issues.

I came down on the social/economic side, but Jack Kent's arguments still stick in my mind. He argued that of course the social/economic issues must be addressed, but if this became planning's focus, the theories and evolution of thought about urban design and physical planning would be diminished and might even disappear. Was he right? How many urban designers reside in typical planning departments? How many schools have separate urban design and physical design planning degrees? It does seem to me that urban design has been lost and has certainly not been adequately picked up by the architects or landscape architects.

LESSON 10
Planners have been confused about planning functions for many years.

[†]*The Urban General Plan* by T.J. Kent Jr., APA 1964. Jack Kent passed away in 1998.

11
MANHOLE PLANNING DIRECTORS

One of our professors at Berkeley periodically brought in a Bay Area planning director to address us and share some real world experiences. By and large these were the most boring sessions we had. It seemed to us that a future as a planning director doomed us to being bland and consummate bureaucrats.

There was one exception: Roy Potter, the Fremont Planning Director, who worked as Planning Director for several counties and later spent 20 years as Executive Vice President of San Diegans, Inc., active in revitalization of San Diego's downtown. Potter told us about the use of meandering sidewalks—a new concept at that time—undergrounding of utilities, density bonuses for good design, and how the General Plan was to be cast into the top of city manhole covers. This manhole scheme was used by Le Corbusier in Chandigarh, India. Unfortunately, the Fremont Public Works Director killed this scheme. For many of us, ideas like his kept our juices flowing.

LESSON 11

Planning Directors don't have to be bland. They can even mold the General Plan into city manhole covers.

12
THE POWER OF GRAPHICS

Ohne of our classmates, Joe Kourakis,[†] had a master's degree in architecture and, unlike me, he could draw. As we put together our teams for projects, everyone wanted Joe on their team. He also did the drawings for our weekly student meetings.

Joe's Coffee Hour Drawing

[†]Currently Professor Emeritus of Planning at California Polytechnic State University, San Luis Obispo, California.

One of our projects was to prepare a plan for San Francisco based on doubling its population. I managed to get on a team with Joe and we called our report The Compact Metropolis. For our theme and cover, we used a drawing of the Monolith in Vigeland Park in Oslo, Norway, that I had discovered on my trip to Europe between my first and second years in planning school. The Monolith consisted of nude intertwined bodies from the bottom to the top. Joe recently suggested to me that "we used this obelisk of clamorous humanity to bring out the humor of neophyte student planners involved in the solution of complex urban problems."

Our research idea may or may not have been the best, but the cover graphic certainly sold our report.

LESSON 12
Never underestimate the power of good graphics.

Joe's Vigeland
Park Drawing

28

13
BROWN-NOSED RESEARCH

One of my best classes at Berkeley, taught by Professor Barclay Gibbs Jones,[†] focused on the theory of the urban economy. As part of our coursework, we were each given an author to research, write a report about, and present to the class.

My author was Adna F. Weber, who had written *The Growth of Cities in the 19th Century*, some 62 years earlier, but then dropped out of sight. Professor Jones said this about Weber:

"By far the greatest development in urban theory by an American prior to the 20th century was made by Adna Weber. Not only is his Growth of Cities in the 19th Century *the major American work of its time, but it is also one of the best reviews and syntheses of all work in the western world to appear by the end of the 19th century. . . . Weber made an incredibly great contribution to urban theory. It is the first real contribution by an American and bears comparison with Levasseur and other Europeans."*

Even though I worked hard on the research, I couldn't determine if Weber was dead or alive. Finally, on a hunch, I decided to check out the New York telephone directory and found a listing with his name. Bingo!

[†] He served as a distinguished planning professor at Cornell for 30 years. Barclay passed away in 1997.

He was 90 years old, almost blind, and delighted to give me a personal interview. He sent me a letter and a copy of an original manuscript of his book with the pages still uncut.

My gift of this book to Professor Jones as part of my class presentation assured me of an A in the class. Weber's letter is shown on the following page.

LESSON 13
Creative research is worth doing and can get you an A.

MR. ADNA F. WEBER

85-21 - 114TH STREET

RICHMOND HILL 18, LONG ISLAND, N. Y.

April 12, 1961

Mr. Paul C. Zucker, Berkeley, Cal.

My dear sir:

Thank you for your letter of the 6th bringing such good tidings about "The Growth of Cities". I hope the work merits Professor Jones's commendation of that 62-year-old book.

I was not aware that the book was out of print as I had heard nothing from Columbia since I authorized the second printing many years ago. My son made inquiry and reports that the book is definitely out of print. I have therefore mailed one of my two extra copies to your address and will ask you to turn it over to Professor Jones when it has served its purpose at the seminar meeting of May 4th.

There is not much to add to the personal data appearing in "Who's Who in America," 1943. I was born on a farm and grew up in Salamanca, a village sixty miles south of Buffalo. As a member of a family with seven children I had to make my own way through college. I began by winning the McGraw scholarship in a competitive examination in mathematics and supplemented that stipend by doing newspaper work. In my senior year I gave up my position as campus reporter of the Ithaca "Journal" in order to become President Schurman's private secretary; but I continued to write for the New York "Tribune" and " Evening Post." I also served for one year each on the editorial board of the "Cornell Era" (weekly) and "Cornell Magazine" (monthly).

I began work on the "Growth of Cities" as a graduate student at Cornell, continued it at the University of Berlin on a Cornell travelling fellowship and at Columbia University on a Columbia fellowship and completed it in 1898 while Assistant Registrar at Cornell. It won the Grant Squires prize which is awarded every fifth year by the Columbia political science faculty.

Doubtless the book had something to do with my entrance into state service through the influence of Governor Roosevelt. And I may here state that one of my pleasantest memories is the fact that I enjoyed the confidence of Theodore Roosevelt as well as that of Governor Charles E. Hughes, who later became Chief Justice of the United States.

Very truly yours,

31

14
SHORT-TERM THINKING, LONG-TERM SOLUTIONS

One of our class assignments was to prepare the plan for the San Francisco Bay Area and complete the plan in a two day charette. I found this short time-line forced a lot of creative thinking.

My scheme, shown in the illustration, was based on the likelihood of short work weeks, small families, increase in older people, desire for high density areas of intense personal exchange and activity opportunities as well as a desire for parks, open space, and agriculture.

To this day, I still think my scheme would have been a good approach for the development of the Bay Area. I used this charette idea through the years and found it to be quite successful. The best current example of charettes are the UDAG studies that show how quick studies can help communities highlight key issues and uncover the big ideas, particularly for downtown plans.

LESSON 14
Charettes can help produce the big ideas.

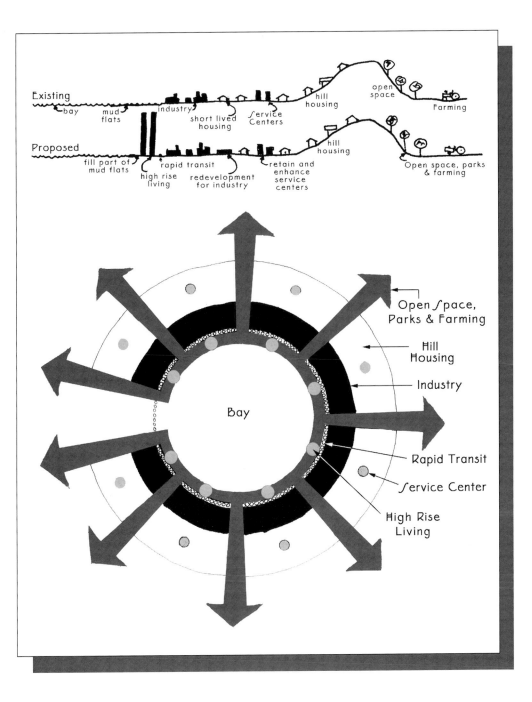

Existing

bay
mud flats
industry
short lived housing
service Centers
hill housing
open space
Farming

Proposed

fill part of mud flats
high rise living
rapid transit
redevelopment for industry
retain and enhance service centers
hill housing
Open space, parks & farming

Bay

Open Space, Parks & Farming

Hill Housing

Industry

Rapid Transit

Service Center

High Rise Living

15
GARBAGE

As planning students we were just as intrigued with technology as today's students, but we had more primitive tools. Computer punch cards and card sorters were our key tools. More advanced students had access to a machine that could easily cross-tabulate the punch cards.

Since I was intrigued with what planners do and think, I decided to do what may have been the first survey of planners in the country. I sent surveys to 278 California planners and published *The Selected Characteristics of Bay Area Planners*. The survey received a lot of state and national attention in the profession. As part of this study I was required to document my costs as shown below.

9"x12" Envelopes	$2.84
3" x 9" Envelopes	$1.66
Post Cards	$1.08
Postage	$8.65
Dittos & Stencils	$2.08*
Paper	$6.00*
IBM Cards	**
	$22.31

* Partially supplied by Department of City & Regional Planning
** Supplied by Survey Research Center

The next semester I needed another research topic and came up with the idea of milking those punch cards for another paper. I titled my new paper, *Supplement to the Selected Characteristics of Bay Area Planners.* Upon receipt of my report, the professor sent me a note asking why I gave him only the supplement to my paper. The paper was good but the use of the word supplement in the title led my professor to assume there was more. This was a good lesson in how words and title can impact people's perceptions.

While working with punch cards one day, a fellow student showed me a technique for verifying the data. Out of curiosity I went back and checked the cards I'd used in my two surveys. Uh oh—a 25 percent error rate. I never did take time to determine how this would have impacted my two reports and no one seemed to challenge my findings.

This experience did lead me to be more careful with data during my planning career. I believe many data errors go undetected in the computer age. I tell my staff if the numbers don't look right, there's a good chance they aren't.

LESSON 15
Garbage in, garbage out, but only if someone catches it.

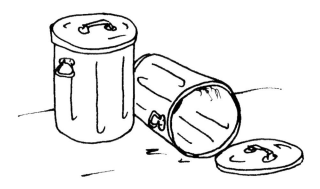

16
EVEN COLLEGE PROFESSORS CAN BE CREATIVE

At the end of two years at Berkeley, we graduate students were given the choice of either writing a thesis or taking a two-day comprehensive exam. All of our class—except one—took the exam option. What this proved was that after two years of graduate school, planning students, in fact, acquire a lot of common sense. I'm not certain that the student who chose the thesis route has yet completed that assignment.

The comprehensive exam was one of the most creative planning tests or documents I've ever seen. We were given a series of historic maps of the San Francisco Bay Area showing development patterns and a listing of key events and dates, i.e., the coming of the railroad, earthquake, gold discovered, and the like. The dates of these events were then changed. Our two-day job was to develop the Bay Area development pattern, population, transportation, and employment that we think would have resulted from the changed circumstances over time. This was sort of Sim City before Sim City. The most important part of the test was to describe, using urban economic theory and land development theory, the rationale for our scheme.

About one-fourth of our class actually failed this exam. Planners should, but often don't understand urban economics and land development theory. Unfortunately, this situation hasn't changed much over the years. Through my planning director jobs and more recent consulting work for planning departments, it's been clear that too few government planners understand the economics of development, and this can create serious problems in community building and city planning.

LESSON 16
To pass muster as a planner, you must understand urban economic and land development theory.

I Passed!

17
MIT BY THE BACK DOOR

I'd wanted to go to MIT for planning school, but wasn't admitted in 1959. Two years later, I applied for a job with the renowned Dean of the MIT Planning School John (Jack) Howard.[†] I was hired to run his Brookline, Massachusetts, consulting staff.

It became a running joke that I was good enough to work for him, but not good enough to be accepted into his academic program. Jack's defense was that through the years, he found it difficult to sort out the best students as well as best employees and how often he was wrong in his selections.

After my own 40 years of hiring hundreds of planners, I have a new appreciation for Jack's thoughts, having made many hiring mistakes myself.

LESSON 17
Hiring those who can and will do the job is one of the most difficult but important jobs a Planning Director must perform.

Jack Howard

[†]Jack Howard passed away in 1995.

38

PART 4

BROOKLINE

18
DON'T CALL ME, WE'LL CALL YOU

In addition to his distinguished career as Dean of MIT's planning program, Jack Howard had a distinguished career as Cleveland's Planning Director in the 1940s. His work included preparation of the Cleveland General Plan, which earned national attention for its broad scope. One of my favorite Howard stories took place when he was readying to leave Cleveland. He was careful to leave various telephone numbers and addresses where he could be reached so the city could call him when it needed help with the transition.

According to Jack, they never called.

LESSON 18
None of us is indispensable.

19
DESIGNING PARKING LOTS

While I may have missed out on Jack Howard's MIT planning classes, I spent four delightful years in Brookline, Massachusetts, learning planning from the master. My first day on the job Jack drew this diagram.

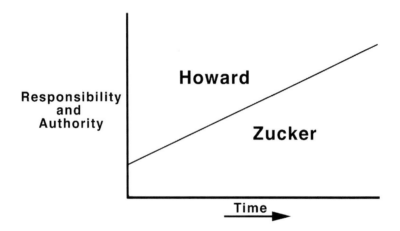

Although he made it clear that my initial responsibilities and authority were small and his were large, his goal was to reverse this as soon as possible. Once a week or so, we would meet for an hour or two and then go to dinner. I rapidly progressed up the chart.

When I teach management today, I make the point that although most planners are trained as operators–technicians, if you are a manager or supervisor, your management tasks must take precedence over other operational tasks since other people in the organization are relying on you.

To make my case, I often describe Jack Howard. He loved to lay out parking lots. If a roll of plans was on the drafting table when he walked in, he would immediately roll them out, pull out a flimsy,[†] and begin to redesign the parking lot. The wrong thing to do? No, in Jack's case he had all of his management tasks fully in tow, so he should be free to do whatever operational tasks he liked to do.

LESSON 19
If designing parking lots turns you on, go ahead and do it, but only after your management tasks are completed.

[†]For the many planners who don't recognize the term flimsy, it is a thin, inexpensive roll of drafting paper often yellow in color.

20
MIKE DUKAKIS FOR PRESIDENT—OR TOWN MEETING MEMBER?

In Brookline, Kathy and I lived several doors down the street from Mike Dukakis. He was living on the top floor of an old Brookline four-story, wooden walkup. I remember sitting on the floor in his living room eating cheese and drinking wine and listening to tales about Democratic politics in Massachusetts. At the time, he was considered a young Turk working with others like him to take over or reform the Democratic party in Massachusetts. He succeeded, of course, later becoming governor and then the Democratic nominee for president. One of his stepping stones was a more modest election as one of 250 members of the Brookline Town Meeting. I always had the impression he wanted me to get involved politically, but I decided that as the town planner, I should stay politically neutral.

LESSON 20
Planning is involved with political issues but planners should not be involved in politics.

(I later created an exception to this lesson as described in Chapter 56.)

Mike Dukakis, upper left; Paul Zucker, lower right.
A committee meeting for the Brookline Community
Renewal Program.

21
HISTORY REPEATS ITSELF

My Brookline office was on the balcony of a 100-year-old town hall that was built before telephones were in use. This...

...was replaced by this

LESSON 21

Revisit lesson 6.

22
NAME YOUR STREET

Working in Brookline presented a whole group of new issues I had not seen before. Brookline is an old city with typical street patterns and street names often found in older cities. One of the first things I discovered was that you could be on what appeared to be the same street and it changed names every few blocks. For example, Cypress Street became School Street and then became Aspinwall Avenue. As a rational planner and a good midwesterner, this made no sense to me whatsoever.

What should be done? Try to rename these segments so the entire length of the street had one name? Wrong. If you want to get into trouble as a planner, try to mess with people's street names, particularly in an old city. This idea was dead on arrival. Fortunately, I didn't die with it.

LESSON 22
Don't mess with established street names, even if they are confusing.

23
WHAT? A USEABLE GENERAL PLAN?

Shortly before I arrived in Brookline, the town had adopted a new General Plan. It consisted of 16 pages and three maps for a town of 61,000 people. All of the background information and documentation were contained in separate sections totaling 31 pages. One could actually look at this document and learn what policy direction the town had decided to take.

Ever since, I've worked with the idea that short is better than long; simple is better than complex; clear and explicit is better than vague and ambiguous. But it's not been easy. Planning law, the courts, and citizens' pressures have tended to bloat the plan. As a consultant, I analyzed the Los Angeles County General Plan, which topped out at 36 inches thick and many volumes.

The San Diego County Plan was a two-volume, eight-inch-thick document. At my farewell party in 1982, the San Diego County staff gave me an ax and I ceremonially "trimmed" the plan.

I've had some successes and some failures along the path of trying to keep things simple. But one stands out in my mind. For one of my consulting firm's APA–award winning plans, we reduced a small city's plan from approximately three inches to one-half inch thick.

LESSON 23

Make little plans. People may actually understand them.

48

Cutting the General Plan down to size.

24
FIRE, FIRE, FIRE

We weren't building many new streets in Brookline, but one of my goals was to keep the engineers and Fire Department from widening many of Brookline's quaint, pedestrian streets or adding large cul-de-sacs or turn arounds on dead-end streets.

My office window faced one of the town's old fire stations that was bounded by one of those narrow streets, maybe 24 feet wide. I used to amuse myself by watching the large fire ladder trucks pull out of the fire station and make a sharp U-turn up that narrow street. And every day, as I watched, the Fire Department unknowingly made my case. They really could maneuver their trucks in very small and tight spaces.

Narrow Street Next to Fire Department

LESSON 24
Don't believe everything the engineers and fire departments tell you. Narrow streets do work.

25
OLD NEW URBANISM

We lived in a Brookline neighborhood that beat anything today's new urbanists are building. Although the area was zoned for multifamily development, it had developed as a single-family area and was then a mixture of single-family, two-family, and multifamily dwellings. Everyone in the neighborhood could walk to school or a park, to any of three trolley lines running to downtown Boston, to churches, shopping and—for the only time in my career—I walked to work in 10 minutes.

One of my favorite walking streets passed a delightful two-family house that I thought would be my ideal house to own. Some years later, I found out Michael Dukakis bought it and I believe still lives there today.

Brookline managed to save many of these old neighborhoods by downzoning them to preserve the mix of housing types. This mix of housing types is virtually impossible to create today.

LESSON 25
Properly executed, the old new urbanism works.

26
THIRTY YEARS AND COUNTING

In my consulting practice I'm continually amazed at how many planning departments continue to use manual logs and similar manual statistics or listings. This is the age of spreadsheets and databases that will run on $700 PCs. There's no excuse for this type of manual activity.

It reminds me of an event that occurred in Brookline over 30 years ago. The Town Clerk kept detailed data on every household in Brookline. These data were printed every year in a large book that included each citizen's name, birthdate, political registration, occupation, move in the last year, all the way to how many dogs there were in the family.

This was all handled manually and thus, it was close to impossible to obtain useful information for planning purposes. While we didn't have PCs or handy databases, we did have access to mainframes that could readily handle this type of task. I began to poke around and explore the option of computerizing this data.

One day, the Chief Administrative Officer called me into his office. He had never seen the usually calm and complacent Town Clerk, who had been on the job for 40 some years, so angry. And all because of that young, whippersnapper planner sticking his nose into the Clerk's manual logs. Needless to say, the logs were not computerized—at least not until 10 years later, long after I had left the scene.

LESSON 26
Examine your logs to see if you, too, are 30 years behind the times.

27
HAVE YOU HUGGED A TREE TODAY?

One of our projects in Brookline was to revitalize commercial areas, mostly by adding parking lots. One such site had a large tree in the middle, which of course, the engineers proposed to remove. I came close to standing in front of the bulldozer to save this tree and, fortunately, eventually found a member of the Board of Selectman, Mrs. Louise M. Castle, to join me in the cause to save the tree.

This was some 35 years ago. Two years ago, I went to visit my tree. How proudly it stands in what would have been two more parking spaces.

LESSON 27
Tie yourself to a tree, then visit it occasionally to let it know that you still care.

With My Tree

28
ORDINANCE FOLLIES

One Brookline job was to write and push through a new zoning bylaw. Both proved to be interesting tasks. I'd never written a zoning bylaw before, but Jack Howard had a clear idea on how he wanted to proceed. He wanted a format that at the time was unique, but today is common. There were separate chapters for use regulations, dimensional requirements, and administrative regulations. The uses were covered in one large matrix table and the dimensional requirements in another large matrix table. There were numerous subsections that seemed to modify everything.

While the use tables worked fairly well, the dimensional requirements were another matter. Many of the dimensions were based on formulas that were combinations of relationships between height and length. Typical formulas would be $\frac{H+L}{6}$ or $\frac{10+H}{10}$.

The Building Department was responsible for administering the bylaw, but once adopted it was clear that it was beyond their capabilities—or one could say the bylaw was unclear. I became the interpreter of the code, answering numerous questions every day. For every question I thought we would answer right, someone found two other places in the code that seemed to modify or nullify our answer.

The dimensional requirements and formulas also were a challenge. While on the surface they seemed to make sense, developers continued to propose buildings that we felt were unacceptable. We speculated that they must have used computers to maximize use of the formulas.

To this day, I still find ordinances that are hard to administer and lend themselves to many staff mistakes. One would think that computer technology would allow some planning departments to say: "Oh, you're in the R3 Zone. Here is a printout of all the regulations that impact you."

LESSON 28

Zoning can be too complicated and often is—keep it simple, stupid (KISS).

District	Minimum Yard[4] (feet) Front	Side	Rear
M-0.5	15	7½	30
	15	7½	30
		none[1,5]	30[5]
	$\frac{H+L^7}{6}$ but at least 15	10	30[5]
M-1.0	15	7½	30
	15	7½	30
		If Height is: under 35 ft. : none[5]	30[5]
	$\frac{H+L^7}{6}$ but at least 15	If Height is: 35-45 ft. : $10+\frac{L}{10}$; over 45 ft. : $\frac{H+L^6}{6}$	$\frac{H+L^6}{6}$
M-2.0	10	7½	30
	10	7½	30
		If Height is: under 35 ft. : none[5]	30[5]
	$\frac{H+L^7}{6}$ but at least 10	If Height is: 35-45 ft. : $10+\frac{L}{10}$; over 45 ft. : $\frac{H+L^6}{6}$	$\frac{H+L^6}{6}$
M-3.0	10	7½	30
	10	7½	30
		If Height is: under 45 ft. : none[5]	30[5]
	$\frac{H+L^8}{6}$ but at least 10	If Height is: 45-60 ft. : $10+\frac{H}{10}$; over 60 ft. : $\frac{H+L^6}{6}$	$\frac{H+L^6}{6}$
M-4.0	10	7½	30
	10	7½	30
		If Height is: under 45 ft. : none[5]	30[5]
	$\frac{H+L^8}{6}$ but at least 10	If Height is: 45-85 ft. : $10+\frac{H}{10}$; over 85 ft. : $\frac{H+L^6}{6}$	$\frac{H+L^6}{6}$

Formulas

29
SELLING ZONING AT A WAKE

Brookline, with a population of 59,000, is the largest community in New England with a modified town meeting form of government. It was modified so that 250 representatives were elected by districts within the town. Any zoning bylaw, ordinance, or map had to be approved by this large and diverse group of people.

We knew that selling a new zoning bylaw would be difficult, particularly the new dimensional requirements. We hired three students who spent an entire summer building three-dimensional models that illustrated what could be built under the existing bylaws and how much better things would be under the new bylaw. The models were all housed in neat, fold up carrying cases so that we could readily do a show and tell. Today I assume we would be doing the same thing on the computer.

We would go from neighborhood meeting to neighborhood meeting, often with a planning commissioner in tow. One meeting particularly stands out in my mind. We knocked on the door and were politely ushered into the living room, where a number of people were already assembled. We sat for a time waiting for the meeting to start and it slowly dawned on us. We were at a wake. Our meeting was in the house next door.

Jack Howard, the Dean of MIT's planning school and

my boss, took the lead at the town meeting where the bylaw was up for adoption and again proved what a teacher he was. He was a short man, maybe just over five feet, but had a major presence. He would answer questions in a straightforward, factual way and never take the barbs or criticisms personally. He was the consummate professional. Between Jack's presence and our diligent homework, the complex bylaw passed with some votes to spare.

LESSON 29

Even a mob can adopt complex zoning documents when handled professionally and your homework is done well.

30
DROWNING IN DATA

In 1954 the federal government created Title I, Section 701, a funding program that provided 50-50 federal-local funding grants for planning in communities of under 25,000 people. By 1960 this program was expanded to make matching funds available to virtually all communities. This 701 program created many comprehensive plans—some good, others just to spend money and employ planners. Another interesting federal funding source created in 1959 was called the Community Renewal Program (CRP). The idea here was that rather than conduct redevelopment projects on a piecemeal basis, the entire city should be considered and a comprehensive, integrated program developed.

CRP had substantial amounts of money, so many of us, including Brookline, signed on. We were like kids in a candy store—gorging ourselves on treats. We could hide all sorts of studies using these funds. We were able to hire Kevin Lynch to conduct the first city-wide application of his urban design theories.[†]

Having become enamored with the computer, and with these funds, we put together the most extensive database I've seen—even to this day—on every property in Brookline. Four or five students worked for three months over the summer conducting field studies. We gathered property sizes, building sizes, number of floors, building materials, categories for struc-

---

[†]Incidentally, this study, although interesting, didn't seem to lead us anywhere. At times I've wondered if a clear, visual image would be public housing that looked like public housing.

tural issues, paint condition, etc. With all this data, our theory went, we could construct the ultimate rational redevelopment model. We had the data, and we constructed numerous models. But each time we took the findings out to the field, we seemed to have crazy results that didn't make sense. As our time and funding ran out, we did what every creative planner does: decided on redevelopment areas based on our gut instincts and judgments and made the data fit.

LESSON 30

Planners may be smart, but not always as smart as we think we are.

31
BROOKLINE—EVEN SHORTER STORIES

HOW TIMES HAVE CHANGED

Several other images stick out in my mind about my Brookline days:

DEEP PURPLE

These were the days before the Xerox machine, and daily work was completed with carbon paper or ditto machines. Both left you covered with purple ink. My secretary's typewriter and desk often looked like a purple cloud had descended on them.

THE COUNTER IS GOOD FOR MORE THAN ACCEPTING PLANS

In the 1950s and 1960s it was not unusual for developers to present planning and building staff with modest gifts. In Brookline, not only did we receive a bottle of booze at Christmas from our customers, it might be a full case left on the front porch. During the Christmas and New Year holiday season, the building permit counter resembled a bar, with open bottles everywhere. It was very festive since the counter was in a three-story-high ceiling room that once was the grand meeting hall of the over 100-year-old town hall.

Although I never personally saw it, we had heard that

some cities printed a list of special fees (tips to employees) that was kept under the counter. One did not need to pay these fees, but it sped up the process considerably. Fast forward to today and those communities that provide accelerated plan checks if employee overtime is paid. The more things change, the more they stay the same.

WHICH COUNTRY?

Neither Boston nor Brookline was particularly integrated and Brookline had mostly Caucasian faces. I was fortunate to have one of the best secretaries ever, Arlene Warner, who happened to be black. Occasionally I would take her to meetings so she could see how her work fit into the whole process. We were working on a high school expansion one time, and Arlene joined me for a meeting with the superintendent of schools. While sitting in the waiting room and making small talk, the receptionist inquired as to what country Arlene was from. I was aghast at this comment but my secretary and I just raised our eyebrows and let it pass. We have made some progress through the years.

LESSON 31
Nothing particular, I just like these stories.

32
SO YOU WANT TO MEET LADY BIRD JOHNSON?

After about four years in Brookline, I started to scour the country for a new, more exciting challenge. Two job openings caught my eye. One was the Planning Director for Marin County, California; the other, a special assistant to the Director of the National Capital Planning Commission in Washington, D.C.

The latter position was described by the Director as the third leg on a three-legged stool: the Director, the Assistant Director, and myself. I was to be special liaison to First Lady Ladybird Johnson and the National Capital Planning Commission, as well as help the Director with internal department matters. He expressed a lack of confidence in his Assistant Director and assumed I would help him with Assistant Director type activities. While interviewing, the Assistant Director made it clear to me that he thought this new position was not necessary.

Yet, I took the job. What an exciting time in our life. We had a two-year-old son and a four-month-old son, we were moving to the heart of U.S. politics, I would be working with the country's first lady, and I received a nice GSA rating and moving expenses. To top it all off, we scraped together every penny we could find and bought our first house in Arlington, Virginia.

The first two weeks on the job were a shocker. While I could drive to the office in downtown D.C. in 15 minutes on weekends, it took over an hour by bus during the rush commute. Even worse, within weeks of getting settled, the Director called the staff together to announce his retirement. Guess who was announced as his replacement? You guessed it, the Assistant Director.

LESSON 32

Three-legged stools work better with three legs than two. Ask your prospective next boss what his or her next career moves are.

PART 5

WASHINGTON, D.C.

33
CHRISTMAS COMES EARLY

About the same time that my boss retired, I had a call from Marin County, which was finally completing its selection process. Could I fly to Marin for an interview? Tears rolled down my wife's cheeks as she drove me to the airport, with two boys in diapers in the back seat, moving boxes only half unpacked, a new house and in two weeks, Christmas. "Are you crazy?" was never spoken, but communicated nonetheless!

Marin had narrowed the field to two candidates. One was a mature, well-respected planner with a considerable track record. The other was a young, somewhat irreverent special assistant to Ladybird Johnson, whom he had never met.

At the end of the interviews, the County Administrator called both candidates into his office at the same time, a somewhat unique move. He described his analysis process. One candidate was a safe, well-tested choice. The other candidate was a less safe, less tested, but potentially dynamic and exciting choice. Either would work.

For many years prior Marin County had a dynamic Planning Director, Mary Summers, who, along with others, convinced Frank Lloyd Wright to design the Marin County Civic Center. Following Mary's retirement, the county had gone through five years of less exciting and more bureaucratic planning. The CAO decided that the best fit at that point in time was for the dynamic, take-a-risk approach. I was in. I often wonder if he remembered this meeting some years later when he recommended my termination (see Chapter 56.)

LESSON 33
There are no good or bad planners, only those that better fit a particular job, in a particular environment, at a particular time.

I learned this lesson again a number of years later when a headhunter recruited me for the Dallas, Texas, Planning Director's job. After going through all the preliminaries, I didn't even get an interview with the City of Dallas. I called the recruiting firm and they said while I was one of the best planners on the list, they determined that my somewhat confrontational style was all wrong for Dallas. I wouldn't have lasted a month. They were right.

34
IN CASE OF NUCLEAR ATTACK ...

Although I was in Washington for only six weeks, it was long enough to observe some of the foibles of federal government work. Among the stacks of forms and instructions for my employment was a one-page memo telling me how to pick up my paycheck in case of nuclear attack—"go to the nearest post office." I wondered if my nearest post office would be somewhere in South Dakota.

I hadn't paid much attention as I was signing, but one form stated if I left before one year, I had to pay back my moving expenses. This was particularly painful since we had adopted the "Oh well, the government is paying anyway" mindset and moved everything from Brookline but the kitchen sink. I took my first and only paycheck and endorsed it to the moving company. My income had basically been a wash.

Feeling somewhat guilty about this short job stay, I decided to do what I could before I left and produced a report on my observations. I found that the review and approval of Planning Commission minutes or letters went through six different reviews, including that of legal counsel.

LESSON 34
How many bureaucrats does it take to proof Planning Commission minutes or write a letter? Six if you're in Washington, D.C.; one or two everywhere else.

You may be wondering if my marriage survived this move and whatever happened to that first house we bought. Our realtor felt very bad for us and suggested we try first to sell it ourselves to avoid the sales commission. She said she'd help us do it and would then list it if we had no luck. Our newspaper ad came out on Christmas morning. Moving boxes were still half-unpacked, amid Christmas wrapping and toys spread around the house. We were still in bed when the phone rang at 7 a.m.; "Can we see the house?" "Of course, come right over."

When my wife drove me to the airport to fly to Marin County interview she thought I was crazy. When I invited someone to look at our messy house at 9 a.m. on Christmas morning she knew it was true. The prospective purchasers were an older couple who had just gotten married and had been interested in the house before we bought it. The fun part was that our realtor recently had been dating the new husband. We sold the house at the end of the meeting for the same price we paid six weeks earlier. And, oh yes, we're still married.

The House—Bought and Sold in Six Weeks

PART 6

MARIN COUNTY

35
OUT OF BODY EXPERIENCE

Marin County, like Washington, had agreed to pay our moving expenses. Fortunately, while I was in Marin for the interview, I had managed to rent a house, designed by renowned architect Mervin Eichler, and had obtained a floor plan of the house.

We left Arlington while the movers were still packing the van. We scheduled stopovers in Nebraska and Minnesota to visit family, causing our furniture to arrive in California before we did.

However, we had marked all the boxes and furniture to correspond to locations on the floor plan that we had given to the movers. We arrived in California at midnight in a rainstorm with the two babies, opened the front door, turned on the lights, and wow! Everything was in place. My wife calmly walked into the boys' room, put the sheets on the cribs and we began to settle in. (This was almost an out of body experience.)

LESSON 35

Planning works.

36
ADVERTISE LIKE CORPORATE AMERICA

If you want to have the best planning department, you should hire the best planners. But, how do you find them and how do they find you? An important tool used by corporate America is advertising. Unfortunately, most governments rely on dry job ads placed in newspapers or professional journals. One successful technique we used in Marin was the job ad shown on the facing page.

This ad attracted a group of high-quality applicants. The picture showed existing staff members. (I'm the guy wearing the tie in the middle.) To illustrate how typical government bureaucracy reacts, several years later when several Board of Supervisors members wanted to fire me, one of them pulled out this old job ad as an example of my bad judgment.

LESSON 36
Eagles don't flock, you have to find them one at a time.

PRINCIPAL PLANNER, ADVANCE PLANNING $12,696 - $15,432 DEPENDING UPON EXPERIENCE. MASTER'S DEGREE IN PLANNING PLUS THREE YEARS EXPERIENCE. ADMINISTRATIVE SKILLS A MUST. WILL BE IN CHARGE OF CO-ORDINATING INNOVATIVE COUNTY-WIDE PLANNING PROGRAM.

CURRENT OR ADVANCE PLANNERS, $10,188-$12,396 DEPENDING ON EXPERIENCE. MASTER'S DEGREE IN PLANNING. CURRENT PLANNER TO WORK ON PLANNED COMMUNITIES, DESIGN REVIEW, SUBD., PROJECTS. ADVANCE PLANNER TO WORK ON HOUSING STUDIES, ECONOMIC STUDIES, AND SOCIAL PLANNING.

Staff of 28 working in incomparable living environment surrounded by bay and ocean, 15 minutes from San Francisco 30 minutes from the University of California at Berkeley. Apply to Paul C. Zucker. Planning Director, Frank Lloyd Wright Civic Center, San Rafael, California 94903.

BEAUTIFUL PEOPLE—WITH BEAUTIFUL THOUGHTS

Creative Job Ad

37
THE PICK OF THE CROP

Having made the decision to reinvigorate its planning program, Marin County authorized me to hire six or seven new planners, including two deputy directors. We had good salaries and Marin was considered a desirable place to live and work. One of my first recruiting stops was at a national planning conference job fair where planners were lined up 12-deep to talk to me. We tried a few techniques that proved helpful.

• I brought along a Polaroid camera and took a picture of every person I interviewed. When I later sat down to review the applicants, these pictures helped me relate my notes and resumes to the personality as well as conversations that didn't make it into my notes. The pictures showed the person exactly as I saw them, including the clothes they were wearing, helped considerably.

• Not being able to fly everyone to Marin for an interview, the county instead flew me to six cities around the country to do interviews at airports.

• Since we were concerned about writing skills, we handed each candidate a blank pad and sent them off somewhere for 15 minutes to write on a given topic. This rapidly cut down our list of candidates. We even had some seasoned planners who brought back a blank pad.

• In the office we had a tote board. Each applicant was placed on a 3-by-5 card and tacked below one of the vacant positions. Those tacked the highest on the board were our leading candidates, but positions shifted as we continued the process.

• The one position we were having trouble with was an urban designer. We finally hired a new graduate of Penn's Urban Design program, sight unseen. Daryl Connybear, an Australian, proved to be an excellent choice.[†]

The result of all the above were some of the finest planners with whom I've ever worked. They were:

Al Solnit, author of *Project Approval, What Do I Do Next?*, *The Job of the Practicing Planner*, and *The Job of the Planning Commissioner*, from New Mexico. One of the most creative planners I ever worked with. He passed away in 1987.

Werner Von Gundell, a German planner who at the time was working in Connecticut. He later became planning director for Marin and then Oceanside, California.

Daryl Connybear, from Australia, a true urban designer.

Wayne Moody, an architect and urban designer, who later went on to be Planning Director for Laguna Beach, California, and Tucson, Arizona.

LESSON 37
Good programs recruit good staff.

[†]Daryl's wife, Leaf, was also interesting. One evening we had the Connybears and two other couples over for dinner. Wanting to be a good host, I bought four cigars "for the men to smoke after dinner." (And you thought cigars were only now becoming popular.) Leaf was sitting to my right. As I went to pass a cigar to her husband, she took it and immediately lit up. My first lesson in sexual discrimination left me without a smoke.

38
FIRST IMPRESSIONS

Planners need to know who holds the power in their community and then work with that power. In Marin, one of the key organizations was the Marin Conservation League. It had been formed many years earlier and counted among its members people who could find the money (often their own) to rescue a threatened piece of real estate as well as many of the county's yuppies, though not yet referred to by that name.

Early in my tenure I was asked to deliver the address at the league's annual meeting (the word speech would be too mundane for this event). The address was a success and this started a friendship that saw me through many tough times in Marin.

The local newspaper (*Pacific Sun*, March 16, 1966) covered the speech this way:

A Shower of New Concepts for Planning in Marin
by Tom Yarish

Applications for the position "ThinkerConsultant," a new breed of planner, were welcomed by new Planning Director Paul Zucker speaking before the 32nd annual Marin Conservation League dinner at College of Marin Friday. Supervisor Byron Leydecker, introducing Zucker as the pride of the Board of Supervisors, commented "We feel we got the right candidate. Furthermore, he's a neighbor of mine," drawing laughter and applause from the 400 conservationists.

Zucker demonstrated a colorful sense of humor and an adroit mind as he addressed the dinner on the topic "Conservation of the Human Spirit," perhaps better labeled "Meet Paul Zucker." "The emphasis is on innovation and research. You will see more of this in my budget, Mr. Leydecker," said Zucker. "We will look for new answers to suburb planning. The old ones won't do."

The county, behind in modern technology, should consider the use of computers now available for the job, he said. The small area master plans are reasonably good, but good civic architecture, subarea design, and under ground utilities will not alone insure the desired future of Marin still suffering old problems.

"Apartment design is bad in my opinion. They won't be livable in the future." Too many of Marin's new homes are built for upper-income families, he said.

A task force for the proper development of Highway 101, Marin's backbone, moderate-income housing implemented with bonus densities for low rent developments, an action program for Richardson Bay, and a study of the area around the Civic Center were suggested by Zucker.

"We can't be at all sure of success, there are failures all across the country. We will need open minds. We can't always use old solutions," he said.

LESSON 38
Find your natural supporters, and make a good first impression.

Marin County's Weekly...

Pacific Sun

AND TAMALPAIS TIMES

SAN RAFAEL, CALIF., WEDNESDAY MARCH 16, 1966
Year 3 Issue 158   1817-4th St.   Phone 456-2402 $7.50 Yr.   10¢ copy

'CONSERVATION OF THE HUMAN SPIRIT' was the keynote address of Paul Zucker, Planning Director of Marin County, at Marin Conservation League's annual meeting Friday night in the new student center at College of Marin. "The result of technological forces, of increased leisure, of increased wealth, is to threaten every place that is separate and distinct," Zucker said, and then outlined what he hopes Marin will do. "Can Marin County survive, or will it go the way of other areas across the country?" he asked. See pages 3 and 6

We Made the Front Page

39
WHY CAN'T YOU BE LIKE ME?

In *My Fair Lady*, Professor Higgins musically wonders why women can't be more like men. If you're a manager, it's easy to wonder why everyone can't be more like you.

Through the years, I've worked with many diverse styles and personalities. One of the more interesting of these was a planner I hired as my Deputy Director for long-range planning, Al Solnit. I credit him with many of the creative ideas we generated in that program. Although he was brilliant, he was a terrible manager. On numerous occasions, I had to intervene between my deputy and his staff. I enrolled him in a management class, but after the first two sessions, the instructor intervened to tell me I had an employee with a management problem. I constantly struggled to balance his assets with the management problems he created.

In the final analysis, we managed to hold things together, and the community benefited from his many talents.

LESSON 39

Good managers learn how to best use diverse personalities.

40
TELL ME WHAT YOU WANT TO DO

My experience with city and county attorneys through the years has led me to believe that most are not helpful. They're quite good at telling you what you can't do, at holding up documents while they research and at times meddling in the planner's domain. As a consultant, I often advise city and county planning departments to stop asking their attorneys for so many opinions. The average planner, with a bit of study, should be capable of answering most of the legal planning issues.

The one exception to poor attorneys in my career was the Marin County attorney, Doug Maloney. Not only was Doug a good attorney, but he was also an accomplished actor. Doug's view of his job was, "Tell me what you want to do and I'll tell you how you can do it."

LESSON 40
Don't ask your
attorney so
many questions,
unless your
attorney is Doug
Maloney.

41
PROGRESSIVE WORDS, CONSERVATIVE ACTIONS

In the '50s and '60s, California elected officials had it both ways. They often approved dynamic, progressive, and proplanning comprehensive or general plans. At the same time, they would approve antiplanning zoning ordinances and specific development activities in total contradiction to the adopted plans.

This nonsense came to an end in California in 1970 when the courts declared that the general plan and implementing ordinances had to be consistent. This action panicked many elected officials, and there were as many plan changes as there were implementing ordinances changed to match the plans. Interestingly, after almost 30 years, the California courts are still handling numerous cases where the zoning ordinance and the plan are inconsistent.

LESSON 41
Watch what you write, you just might get it (or the judge might give it to you anyway).

42
WHAT'S IN A NAME?

One of our planners, Al Solnit, who headed advanced planning, had a wonderful way of turning a phrase. These phrases tended to garner our reports more attention than they otherwise would have generated. For example:

Can the Last Place Last
(a report on the environmental
quality of Marin)

Don't Leave It to Elsewhere
(a report on housing issues)

Enough for Everyone
(another report on housing issues)

There were times later in my career when I forgot this lesson, but when I did remember it, it always served me well.

LESSON 42
Imaginative phrases can help you sell ideas.

43
THE CHECK'S IN THE DESK DRAWER

Most government staff departments (personnel, budget, attorney, and information technology) are designed to control or keep you from doing something rather than give you support. Through the years, I found a variety of creative techniques to circumvent these departments.

One I most vividly remember took place in Marin County. I discovered that we could use salary savings to hire temporary employees. While the temporary employees theoretically should have been in the permanent job's salary range, there was no absolute written requirement that they be so. I hired a $100-an-hour training consultant using clerical salary savings. I completed the course, processed the payment, and had the check in my desk drawer ready to give to the consultant on his next trip to town.

The personnel director had gotten wind of my approach and stopped by to tell me I couldn't do this. I casually pulled the check out of my desk drawer to show him that not only could I do it, I already did.

This little caper didn't enhance my relationship with the personnel director and I paid for it many times over in other personnel transactions. It was a clear pyrrhic victory: I won the battle, but lost the war. But it sure did feel good at the time.

LESSON 43
Be creative, but be careful of pyrrhic victories.

44
PUT YOUR MONEY WHERE YOUR MOUTH IS

The chairman of Marin's Board of Supervisors was president of a local bank. One day he suggested that if I wanted to buy a house, to let him know. Since we had eaten up our savings in the Washington, D.C., fiasco, buying a house was furthest from our minds. Until we heard his terms, that was—nothing down and 100 percent financing. We soon bought a contemporary Eichler house nestled in a live oak forest in a lovely valley, Lucas Valley.

The valley was surrounded by magnificent hills that soared some 1,800 feet upward. From the top, one could see magnificent views of San Francisco. The developer had built on the flatter land, but had left some rolling slopes with still readily developable land between the houses and those magnificent hills. Every year or two, a developer would show up wanting to develop that land and the residents would fight them off.

One year I suggested to our neighbors that rather than continue to fight the developers, we could cooperate to buy all the land to the top of the hills. We bought 285 acres using 30-year bonds. Eighty percent of the residents voted on this issue with a nearly unanimous, 96 percent favorable vote. This launched a movement in Marin, in which other neighborhoods took a similar approach that today has preserved 4,487 acres of permanent open space.

Part of the purchased open space

Last year I was surprised to receive an invitation to a mortgage burning. The 30-year bonds had been paid off.

LESSON 44
Citizens will rise to the occasion once they see the way.

45
FRANK LLOYD WRIGHT LESSONS

Marin County government is housed in an extraordinary civic center designed by Frank Lloyd Wright. Marin is filled with stories about how this happened.

Marin County Administration Building

• Mary Summers, former planning director, followed Wright out of a stormy Board of Supervisors meeting—where he was called a Communist among other slurs—and convinced him to continue with the project.

• Supposedly, Wright visualized his design bridging the hills immediately upon his first visit to the site. When he toured the site he was told "the county could level anything you want leveled." "Don't you level anything!" snapped Wright. "I need it all. I'm going to use these knolls just the way they are. I can see it now."[†]

• While dining at Summers's house, he sat in a chair and waved his cane directing her and her husband to rearrange the living room furniture to better fit the unusual shape of their living room. Commenting on their leaking roof, he said, "Don't worry about it, most of my buildings leak too."

• At one point, construction stopped and the Board of Supervisors considered turning the partially built civic center into a hospital.

The design of the Frank Lloyd Wright County Administration Building allowed considerable informal contact with other county employees. Unlike a high-rise building, when you walked out of your office, you would see other employees across the courtyard, on the balconies or down the long terraces. I could corner and challenge the county engineer in this informal setting, whereas I might have had trouble confronting him in a formal meeting setting.

LESSON 45
Good design can be hard to come by, but can change the way we behave.

[†] From *Vera, First Lady of Marin,* Hilltop Publishing, 1998

46
PLANNING WITH S&H GREEN STAMPS

When I was growing up, S&H green stamps were popular items dispensed by many grocery stores and other businesses. Stamps were pasted into books, and when you had enough books, you could turn them in for merchandise. My mother let me be the keeper of green stamps and I would use them to do my Christmas shopping.

It may have been this history that gave me the idea of proposing a green stamp approach to planning the undeveloped parts of Marin County. We called this Yield Point Theory. The idea was a takeoff on what eventually became the concept of transfer of development rights. Our approach was based on the following six concerns about undeveloped area general plans:

1. They rapidly become obsolete. The plans seem unable to shift with changing assumptions, values, technology, and forecasts.

2. They fail to recognize that due to rapidly advancing technology, the accuracy of speculation about the future is reduced geometrically as we move away from today and toward "year x."

3. The use of a plan map showing fixed locations for facilities and land use assumes a greater degree of land and economic analysis than has actually taken place.

4. Inadequate collection and analysis of ecological factors is common. Such material, properly developed, is valuable for any plan concept. Inordinate

amounts of time are spent on portions of the plan that can quickly become outdated rather than on the more lasting and useful elements.

5. Unearned economic values that are either created by the plan or by public facilities proposed in the plan, are given to the property owner who happens to be in the right location. In comparison, other owners are penalized.

6. The usual assumption that the necessary power and politics for implementation will be available is often unrealistic. Attention to implementation techniques and realities needs to be an integral part of the plan-making process.

Our idea was simple. Each property owner would be issued yield points equivalent to a number of green stamps. We would use current assessed value as a basis for issuing points. The higher assessed values would be issued the most points and vice versa. Then we would assign required number of points for each type of land use. For example, a single-family house might require one point, a duplex two points, and a shopping center 50. The idea was if the numbers were properly assigned, large areas would remain in agricultural and open space and any unearned increment would accrue to the public.

We got so far as to present the idea to the Planning Commission. While some members were intrigued, I left Marin County before we could test this idea further, and it eventually died.

LESSON 46
Transfer of development rights concepts could be used to build an entire plan implementation system for relatively undeveloped areas.

47
UNDERSTANDING AGRICULTURE

The relationship between planners and farmers in Marin was tense at best. The farmers thought we were out either to overregulate them or to zone away their future development rights.

As part of our continued dialogue with the faculty at Berkeley, we became acquainted with Robert Twiss. He had ideas about looking at the land in different ways. Through a grant from the America the Beautiful Fund and some of our funds, he produced a report called, *Nicasio, Hidden Valley in Transition*. His was a unique approach at the time because it looked in detail at topography, geology, soil, hydrology, climate, vegetation, wildlife, and visual characteristics.

I still remember presenting this report to the agricultural community one evening in a rural meeting hall packed with angry farmers. As the evening unfolded, the mood began to shift. For the first time, the farmers who loved their land were hearing from a planner who also seemed to understand and appreciate the land. A first connection had been made.

The study, along with many other activities, eventually led to the acceptance of agricultural preservation in Marin. The entire story of saving family farms in Marin was detailed in *Farming on the Edge* by John Hart, University of California Press, 1991.

LESSON 47

Understand the land if you want to preserve agriculture.

Many years later in San Diego County, we violated
this principle. See Chapter 98.

NICASIO

HIDDEN VALLEY IN TRANSITION

48
FLEXIBLE PLANS

After Frank Lloyd Wright died, there were future buildings to be completed by the Frank Lloyd Wright Foundation. The Marin planning department was given the task of working with the foundation on a master plan. In projecting the future, we suggested that the one thing we could be certain about was that any prediction of government floor space needs would be wrong. Thus, we pushed for a flexible master plan approach that could accommodate both a low-space projection as well as a high-space projection. This proved to be a concept totally alien to the foundation and, as I have learned since, most architects, as well as planners.

LESSON 48

Since the future is uncertain, we should develop flexible plans.

49
ACTS OF GOD

Marin County is home to the San Andreas fault. After the Planning Commission approved plans for a brick church with a brick steeple sitting directly on top of the fault, we decided another approach might be called for.

The San Francisco Bay Area was filled with earthquake experts and the Geologic Services national office was nearby in Menlo Park. Since in the '60s California cities and counties hadn't yet addressed earthquake issues, it was easy to put together a volunteer committee of some of the country's best geologic scientists who felt the issue needed to be addressed.

To add some weight and prestige to this effort, we decided to have the committee appointed by the Board of Supervisors. The Board turned us down by a three-to-two vote. The chairman of the board said,

"It simply is not in the realm of sensible action to define the acts of God," and then cast his vote with the majority.

LESSON 49
Sometimes it's better not to ask.

50
MAKE NO LITTLE PLANS

Throughout my career, I never got in trouble for the big ideas, only the little ones. My only regrets are the big ideas I didn't think of or put off until too late.

When it came time to write a new Marin County Plan, we came up with one big idea that has stood the test of time. We simply divided the county into three well-defined areas—urban, agricultural, and recreational—and built the General Plan argument around this idea. This was an idea people could understand and support. In 1998 the Marin County Board of Super-visors passed a resolution celebrating the 25th anniversary of this great idea. The big idea stood the test of time.

LESSON 50
Find the big ideas and they will sell themselves.

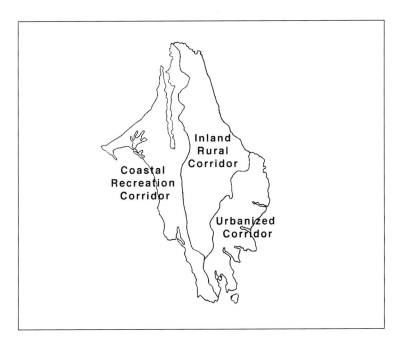

The Simplified Marin County General Plan
Concept

51
MYTHS OF TRANSPORTATION PLANNING

In 1968 I was asked to make a presentation to the California Assembly's Transportation and Commerce Committee on highway planning. At the end of my presentation, I'm certain the members thought I was a bit crazy. I started my presentation this way:

> *"It is a great pleasure when a city planner is invited not only into the forum of transportation planning, but simultaneously into the political arena of a State Assembly Committee. We have been increasingly seeing more and more of this around the state and around the country. It may mean that political and transportation experts have at long last recognized the wisdom of the planning profession and turned to it for advice. On the other hand, it may mean that transportation problems have become so critical that almost anyone is being turned to in desperation. I hope the former but fear the latter."*

I presented what I considered to be five myths about transportation planning:

Myth 1. Transportation Planning Is the Problem
After many long and hard battles, it appears that the concept of balancing all modes in the transportation system is gaining acceptance. Unfortunately, the need for a broader balance is still given only lip service. By broader balance, I mean that a true transportation system must not only balance the automobile with public

transportation, but also must balance transportation systems with land use and other community goals.

Myth 2. Transportation Experts Are Now Considering Social, Economic, and Physical Characteristics of Transportation

Current practices in this area have improved. We are now analyzing proposed facilities for tax impact, relocation problems, division of neighborhoods, provision of landscaping, etc. Such considerations, however, are only a starting point in this area.

a. Today, virtually all transportation facilities are being constructed primarily to meet current traffic movements or movements projected on current experience. While such needs, of course, must receive high priority, of perhaps equal priority should be the construction of facilities to implement broader social, economic, and physical goals. This means it may be desirable to construct a facility to encourage land development where there currently is no traffic demand.

b. Clearly related to (a) above, is how our transportation system relates to the socioeconomic make-up of the community. Properly developed transportation solutions could open up the suburbs to our urban minorities for jobs, recreation facilities, and housing. I am strongly convinced that the great problems of our central cities will require full suburban participation for solutions. On a less theoretical basis, it must be asked: how many of our transportation facilities have dislocated the rich versus the poor; how many have offered positive location advantages to the disadvantaged?

Myth 3. Equal Weight Should Always be Given to Private and Public Transportation

The virtues of the automobile have been extolled time and time again. I agree with all of them. If the automobile is provided relatively free flow during peak hours, it will be selected over and above public transportation. But this argument misses the entire point.

Public transportation must be placed at an advantage over the automobile if many community goals are to be achieved. A system where the automobile is allowed free flow during peak hours will simply not result in a good public transportation system. This has been documented time and time again across the country. We need to think in terms of desirable congestion, both for traffic lanes and parking facilities. Transit can work only where automobile movement is restricted and the automobile's basic advantages are offset by system limitations.

Myth 4. In Terms of New Highways, Construction Freeways Are the Only Efficient Facility to Build

Where freeways are not acceptable, due to either great destruction of existing communities or natural environments, other solutions must be found. No state highway currently exists for Marin's eastwest traffic in the central part of the county, but a freeway is shown on the state system. To date, all Division of Highways proposals have been totally unacceptable to the communities involved. Several interesting alternatives have been suggested, but not explored. For example, three existing, roughly parallel local streets could be improved to expressway standards if they included space for buses. This could conceivably handle the problem at a cost substantially under the freeway proposal and possibly be accepted locally.

Myth 5. New Sources of Funds Are Needed for Public Transportation Systems

It has been a long time since we have seen a truly new source of funds for any public purpose. We need to take an old source—the gas tax—and open up the coffers for public transportation. This obviously does not sit well with the highway lobby, but I suggest it be tried out on the people lobby. Sometimes it appears that the highway lobby is communicating directly with automobiles rather than the people who drive them.

LESSON 51

Automobile congestion can be positive.

52
CONSTITUENCIES ARISE

In 1969, four years after I came to Marin, the County Board of Supervisors started to become more conservative and less supportive of planning. One day I was called into an executive session and three members of the five-member board asked for my resignation. Given the progressive nature of our planning program and the new conservative board majority, my rumor mill told me this might be coming so I had researched the county personnel code and also discussed procedures with the County Counsel.

I told the board that I had no intention of resigning, so they had to resort to termination. I reminded them that I was entitled to a public hearing. They said, "Okay open the door to the chambers and we'll have a public hearing right now." Fortunately the County Counsel advised that this impromptu action would not meet the intent of the statute and it should be an advertised hearing.

That hearing was the largest in the county's history. The standing-room-only crowd testified for nine hours. At the end of the hearing, I was given a three-to-two vote of confidence. One vote had shifted.

How was this possible? Constituency building. We had worked methodically to build a base of support for good planning and, when the chips were down, the constituents rose to the occasion.

LESSON 52
Build your constituency for good planning.
Constituencies that came forward that day in
1969 to support good planning included:

American Association of University Women
American Institute of Planning
Audubon Canyon Ranch
Black Point Improvement Club
City of Belvedere City Council
City of Belvedere Planning Commission
City of Tiburon City Council
Gallinas Village Improvement Association
Kent Woodlands Property Owners Association
Lucas Valley Homeowners Association
Lynwood Park Improvement Association
Marin Council for Civic Affairs
Marinwood Association
Meadowsweet Improvement Association
Muir Beach Improvement Club
Muir Beach Improvement Association
San Anselmo Chamber of Commerce
San Anselmo City Council
San Anselmo Homes Association
Seven San Francisco Architects
Sleepy Hollow Homes Association
Tamalpais Valley Improvement Club

53
BRIDGE BUILDING

Following that hearing, I sent the letter shown on the next page to everyone who attended. I received numerous thank yous from people who had supported my firing.

LESSON 53

Keep on building bridges with those who oppose your ideas.

Marin County Planning Department

Civic Center   San Rafael   California   94903   Telephone   479 1100   Director   Paul C Zucker

4 June 1969

AN OPEN LETTER TO THE PERSONS
INVOLVED IN THE ZUCKER HEARING

May this open letter serve as a means to express my
personal thanks to all those persons who came to my
support and the support of the Planning program in
the recent Board of Supervisors hearing. I particularly appreciate the support of those who may have
differed with us in the past, but share our concern
for honest public debate and those who believe the
program should be continued on this basis.

To those persons who publicly supported my removal
from office, I wish to express my admiration for
standing by your convictions as I truly believe we
share this common desire for holding to convictions.
I would welcome the opportunity to discuss our differences in a calm atmosphere and am at your disposal
in this regard.

In the final analysis, the hearing has shown again
that Marin County is worth getting excited over and
even, if necessary, getting fired over.

Keep up the excitement.

Paul C. Zucker, Planning Director

PCZ cp

DEAR PAUL : THIS IS A BEAUTIFUL STATEMENT.
JUST KEEP ON DOING YOUR THING.
I REMINDED BILL GNOSS BY TELEGRAM THAT YOU
WERE DOING EXACTLY WHAT I HAD URGED HIM
TO HIRE YOU FOR AND WHAT HE HAD AGREED AT THE
TIME TO BE BEST FOR MARIN COUNTY — HOPE THAT IT
HELPED HIM TO VOTE AS HE DID. BEST WISHES, Felix Warburg

54
GOOD NEWS HELPS

Early on in my career I had learned that newspapers, television, and radio like clear, short quips. I also learned that I was good at delivering these. Later in my career, I discovered that it was usually better to let the elected officials have the quips and the air time rather than the bureaucrats.

Irrespective of this issue, it's helpful for the planning director to find friendly press. In Marin County, we had both a progressive, liberal weekly newspaper and a more traditional, conservative daily paper. Early on, the progressive paper seemed to pick me up as a favorite and ran numerous complimentary and positive articles. The conservative paper ran the opposite. One would have thought they were describing two different people or programs.

LESSON 54
Find the friendly press and work with them.

55
BOOTLEG FACULTY

In Marin, we were committed to continuing education of staff. But like most governments, couldn't always obtain the dollars we needed for training.

The University of California, Berkeley, with its Master of City Planning program, had many outstanding faculty members, but there was no way we could enroll our staff in their classes. So we tried another approach. We scouted out the various courses being given, then approached the faculty members to teach the same course on a bootleg basis in our department for a modest fee. The courses were usually held from 4 to 6 p.m. Staff was paid for one hour of the course and asked to volunteer their time for the second hour. We had some excellent courses using this technique.

LESSON 55
Look to your local community for continuing education opportunities.

56
SHOOT THE KING

A year after I was almost fired, I was approached to run against the Chairman of the Marin Board of Supervisors. While I dismissed the idea, at first, the more I thought about it, the more intrigued I became.

One Sunday morning, we hosted a small meeting of influential county citizens in our living room to discuss the idea. Although everyone wanted the incumbent defeated, there was some concern if I could accomplish that, but great support if I decided to run. There was unanimous agreement on one point! If I decided I wanted to run, I shouldn't do it if the group couldn't raise a specific amount of dollars before the filing date. This seemed sensible, so we started the fund raising. By the filing deadline, we had raised only one-third of our goal. What did I do? I filed.

I believe 95 percent of politics is based on ego; obviously mine was alive and well.

Some felt I was running because the chairman of the board was one of the two votes to fire me and clearly a nonsupporter of planning. Although an issue, this was not foremost in my mind. Instead, I thought: When else as a government planner, when else in my career would I have enough name recognition to run for elected office? My firing hearing a year earlier had set the perfect stage.

The Board of Supervisors granted my leave of absence and I was off and running.

And so the campaign started with little money, little knowhow and little preparation. What we lacked in all of these, we made up for with volunteers and creativity.

- Two people, Betty Forry and Morris Kilgore, volunteered as full-time, unpaid campaign managers.

- The well-known California Field Poll did free polling.

- A local architect friend, Cliff Hansen, designed all the graphics and brochures.

- Students silk-screened all of the campaign signs by hand.

- A supporter gave us a discounted rent for a campaign headquarters within a stone's throw of the County Civic Center.

- Malvina Reynolds, songwriter and singer who wrote *Little Boxes*, agreed to give a free benefit concert fund-raiser.

Little boxes on the hillside,
Little boxes made of tickytacky,
Little boxes on the hillside,
Little boxes all the same.
There's a pink one and a green one
And a blue one and a yellow one,
And they're all made out of tickytacky
And they all look just the same.

- Local artists and musicians donated their time and talents for a fund-raiser.

- Dozens and dozens of volunteers answered phones, stuffed envelopes, and put up signs.

- We raised some, but not enough, money.

Several events stand out as being particularly memorable.

• We gave away 10,000 live redwood saplings. They not only reinforced my environmental message, but gave precinct workers something to do and extra comfort in knocking on doors while they delivered the trees.

• Our campaign button had no name on it. The idea was that when people saw it, they would inquire and the answer would reinforce the name.

Campaign Button

• We attracted some conservatives who didn't believe in our cause but hated the incumbent. Overall, I found this a bit hard to deal with.

• I canceled the Malvina Reynolds concert to appease the conservatives. In retrospect, this was one of my biggest mistakes.

• I shaved my beard for one of the few times in my life, another mistake. I needed to be true to myself. It was too late to try to turn myself into a conservative politician.

• Our fund-raising party held at the Unitarian Church was one of the best parties I've ever attended, but almost got the church's nonprofit and non-political status in trouble.

• Much to my surprise, Field Polls showed I had only 19 percent name recognition.

• Although our poll numbers were going up by the day, our campaign ended a few weeks too short. I lost 56 percent to 44 percent.

• This campaign was like an MBA in politics and the loss helped me to re-right my ego.

• I was fired at the first Board of Supervisors meeting following the election.

• The ACLU wanted to file a lawsuit, but my wife and I decided to move on to other things.

• One of my supporters was a young Democratic activist, now U.S. Senator Barbara Boxer.

LESSON 56
If you're going to shoot the king, make certain you hit him.

57
PLANNERS LOVE SIGNS

Finding good places to put up campaign signs was a whole new experience and an adventure. We found one premium spot owned by one of my supporters right on the 101 Freeway. This was the only freeway in Marin County so virtually anyone who traveled in the county had to see the sign. Furthermore, the location was right in the middle of the supervisory district that I was running in.

There was only one problem. Almost as soon as we put up the sign, someone took it down. We didn't know who it was and could never catch them. One night, when returning from a campaign meeting, I stopped to put up a new sign and decided to park in the dark nearby with the hope of catching the culprit. After waiting a half-hour or so, I gave up. As I drove away a police car with flashing lights pulled up behind me and pulled me over. They had received a call about a strange person lurking in the neighborhood and wanted to talk to me. Seeing all my campaign materials in the back seat of my car they accepted my story and let me go on my way.

To this day, we still don't know who was stealing our signs. It could have been supporters of my opponent or perhaps just some planner who didn't like off-premises signs.

LESSON 57
The antisign positions held by many planners should be restrained. Signs can be useful.

58
TOO HOT TO HANDLE

It soon became clear that a Planning Director who takes a leave of absence to run against his Chairman of the Board has a few strikes against him in the planner's job market. In the year before running for office I was continually called by recruiting firms. In the year after, none called.

Finally out of the blue, I was offered a job. Two people who had supported my campaign needed a planner. Don Vial and Mike Peevy both worked for the Institute of Industrial Relations at Berkeley and had offices on the campus. They were both advisers to Cesar Chavez and were interested in California farm worker and labor issues. They had applied for a Federal Office of Economic Opportunity grant to create a nonprofit, lower income community development corporation on the west side of the California Central Valley. The state of California was about to construct a new north/south freeway, Interstate 5, that paralleled the California water canal , a massive federal and state water project that was to rescue the area of large landholders from a diminishing water supply. The idea was to find a way for low-income people to benefit from this major investment rather than be left behind as was customary with most public investment.

Vial and Peevy had received a modest $90,000 grant from the Federal Office of Economic Opportunity, but neither was in a position to manage it. Vial was Chair of the Center for Labor Research and Education, and Peevy had joined Vial as a project specialist with the center. He was also starting a campaign for state senator. I agreed to take the job for a year, provided I could have my office in Berkeley and fly to Fresno as necessary.

LESSON 58
Friends and events often converge at the same time.

PART 7

FRESNO

59
PUT $1 MILLION IN YOUR HAND

Using the initial grant, we created a nonprofit corporation and were selected by the Office of Economic Opportunity (OEO) as a Title I–D program as one of roughly 34 national community development corporations to be funded. These were excellent grants with few strings attached. They could be leveraged on a nine-to-one basis for business creation using SBA loans.

I walked into our neighborhood branch bank with a million-dollar check in my hand. The bank manager stood at attention. Every time my wife walked into the bank on our personal business, she would be embarrassed by the bank manager who would leap out of his chair and warmly greet her.

My leading low-income organizer had no problem obtaining his first ever bank credit card even though his income was that of a welfare recipient.

LESSON 59

Money talks.

60
HIRED GUN

I was an Anglo running a large, low-income Hispanic corporation and I didn't even speak Spanish. Our meetings were held with headphones and simultaneous translation. A perfect situation? Yes.

There was never any doubt about my role in the corporation either by myself or the Board of Directors. I was a hired gun. I neither wanted nor could obtain political power. My role was clear.

LESSON 60
Keeping professional and political roles separate can often be desirable.

**At Board of Directors Meeting
I'm on the left, Leo Placentia, community organizer, is on the right.**

61
WHAT'S IN A NAME ?

Early on, we had to create a name for the corporation. I thought it should be something like the "West Side Development Corporation" that would reflect what we were trying to do. However, our Hispanic board was much more politically astute than I was; they said this name would be read as a threat to the West Side and established local politics. Cesar Chavez was already creating too much stir in the valley. They suggested something less threatening, the "West Side Planning Group." They viewed planning as never accomplishing much and thus not threatening.

I also had my eyes opened when I went to order our stationery. I had always thought of the planning profession as progressive and creative. Upon seeing the name, the stationery store manager said, "Of course you'll want something pretty conservative to fit with planning."

LESSON 61

Unfortunately, planning may not be adequately threatening.

62
FRESNO OR JAIL

With a million dollars in the bank account, the nonprofit corporation was on its way. We hired two full-time organizers, an attorney, a business development expert, and a secretary. I flew into Fresno two days a week and worked at my office in Berkeley the other three days.

Our corporation membership and Board of Directors was made up of mostly low-income Hispanics and a few African Americans. This was the '70s. Our members felt that Nixon was s...ing the country in Washington and our board members couldn't understand why they had to follow federal rules in spending the money. The stated goal of the corporation was to use the money to eventually develop a self-sustaining corporation. Each of my trips to Fresno was an adventure and I had to continually stitch things back together that had fallen apart during my three days in Berkeley.

We were still living in Marin County, the garden spot of the country. We and our friends viewed Fresno as the pits as well as using other descriptive labels. However, I finally said to my wife, only partially tongue in cheek, "We need to move to Fresno or I'll end up in jail." Every week when I traveled to Fresno, I had to undo myriad questionable activities of our members. We moved.

Fresno was not at all as we had envisioned it. We bought a large, 30-year-old contemporary house that the head of the California Democratic Party had once owned. It was obviously much less expensive than the house we left in Marin. Supposedly Stevenson and Kennedy had both been entertained in this house. We had twice the house and a swimming pool for two-thirds the cost of our Marin County house. Our neighbors were great, and we liked the weather most of the time. We described Fresno to our friends as a great place to live, but I wouldn't want to visit there.

LESSON 62
Even the pits can be a good place to live.

63
FISH FARMS

The directors of the Federal Office of Economic Opportunity Community Development Corporations were one of the most interesting groups I've ever belonged to. There were only 34 funded programs throughout the United States. Each of the programs had direct contact to influential U.S. senators and representatives, in our case, Sen. Alan Cranston (D-Calif.) and Rep. Burney Sisk (D-Calif.) of Fresno. The directors would meet at least twice a year to share ideas and coordinate political muscle. Most of the directors were Hispanic, African American, or Native American. As an Anglo hired gun, I was an exception. A few of the programs like ours were rural, but most were urban. Several of these meetings stand out in my memory.

• One of our meetings was held at the Ghost Ranch, about 50 miles northwest of Santa Fe, New Mexico. The ranch, which was depicted by Georgia O'Keefe in many of her paintings, is in a beautiful, but remote setting. After the first day of our meeting, our urban directors were literally climbing the walls for something to do. This may have been the first and last meeting held in a remote location.

• Another trip was to Sparta, Georgia, to visit what was apparently one of the most successful community development corporations. That CDC had a good catfish farming business and had the Ford Foundation providing large annual grants. The CDC had also organized the majority African American residents to out vote the Caucasian minority who had been in political power for many years. We arrived by bus and were given a police escort to the CDC's development complex. The director had the word "slave" embroidered in quarter-inch high letters on his dress shirt as well as on the door of his Lincoln Continental. During our meetings, we kept peppering the director about fish farming and how he had made it such a success. Finally, in desperation, he gave us all a lecture. The real idea, he suggested, was not to be financially successful, for that would eliminate the large foundation and OEO grants. Instead the idea was to always appear that you were about to be successful, thus guaranteeing that next grant.

LESSON 63
At times about-to-be successful is as important as being successful.

64
JUST ASPIRIN

As the various community development programs around the country began to mature, many of them had products to sell and found marketing to be a real challenge. Out of this dilemma came the concept of social marketing. The idea was that many people would buy a product similar to other products on the market if it had a secondary benefit of supporting a social cause. In our case, the social cause was helping low-income people become self-sufficient. Eventually, the idea was to market standard products such as aspirin. Instead of a Bayer or Safeway aspirin, we would sell "Just Aspirins."

However, to begin we had to work with whatever products we had. One person traveled the country to take photographs, write text, and design a catalogue called *Shop the Other America*. In the catalogue, each community development corporation was featured with a brief description. I went to lunch with the author to brief him on our program.

One of our goals in the West Side Planning Group was to eventually become politically active and, in a sense, politically take over portions of the west side of the valley. Obviously, this was not something we wanted advertised and I made it clear in our interview that this was not the way to describe our organization. When the catalogue came out, much to our surprise, it described our program exactly the way I said it shouldn't be described. This was political dynamite and could have sunk our entire effort, funding, and local support.

The catalogues were already printed and some distribution had started. We demanded that for those not yet distributed that the offensive text be cut out of each catalogue and, thankfully, it was done. Then we waited for the negative feedback from those catalogues that were already on the street. It must have been pure luck, but the word never got back to our local community. Or no one read it.

It's interesting to note that the idea of marketing via a social cause never really took off. We sold some of our aprons, pillows, and bike bags via the catalogue, but it certainly wasn't a windfall. It may have been the catalogue, it may have been the distribution, or it may be an idea that simply doesn't work. But someday, if someone tries to sell you a "just product," why not give it a try.

LESSON 64
Be careful of what you say, someone may repeat it.

Cover of the Catalogue

65
CULTURAL INTERCHANGE

In running a low-income economic development corporation, we found that most of the traditional planning ideas or regulations were of little value or interest to our efforts. However, we did brainstorm and try to develop one idea that was unusual.

The State of California and the relevant counties in which the new Interstate 5 freeway was to pass had decided to limit commercial development to only a few interchanges. The area we were working on was to have commercial development at only two of the many interchanges. We developed a concept called the "Cultural Interchange." The idea was to allow commercialization of a third interchange dedicated to enterprises owned and run by low-income people and sponsored by our community development corporation.

We saw the cultural interchange as the beginning of a new community accommodating:

- Growing, display, and marketing of agricultural products
- Health and emergency facilities
- Recreational activities
- Typical freeway-related commercial uses
- A cultural center
- Distribution of Mexican products

We described our concept as follows:

"The West Side of Fresno and Kings Counties is about to experience significant economic development because of the federal-state irrigation projects and the completion of Interstate Route 5. The questions are; will this economic expansion open up new opportunities for the participation of low-income residents and significantly improve their economic status and well-being? Or will the wealth created by such development accrue only to those in and out of the area who command the economic resources and technical assistance necessary to benefit?"

We explored this idea with the county planners with only lukewarm response and soon became preoccupied with other ideas. In retrospect, this was a dynamite idea. I regret not having pulled it off.

LESSON 65
Don't give up too soon on your dynamite ideas; you'll regret it in hindsight.

DUMB IDEAS

By the time I left the West Side Planning Group after four years, we had obtained numerous other federal funds and nonprofit grants and loans and created many subsidiary corporations. We had two attorneys, several community workers, a credit union, a movie theater, a clinic, and five manufacturing plants. Although we were partially successful, we also came up with many dumb ideas.

The dumb ideas are described in Chapters 67, 68, 69, and 70.

LESSON 66
If you're not creating a few dumb ideas, you're not learning.

67
FREEWAY BARRIERS

Our CDC was always looking for new and exciting business ventures. This proved to be a problem. In hindsight, we would have been better off buying a few well-established and growing businesses.

In any case, our business development staff unearthed two guys in Los Angeles who were developing a machine that would extrude the New Jersey type concrete median freeway barriers. Since the federal highway program was in full bloom, this seemed like an exciting concept. The idea was a machine that would simply drive down the freeway medium. Trucks would unload concrete in the front and barriers would magically appear out the back. We bought 51 percent of this venture and moved it to Fresno.

We moved the yet-unfinished machine into a large warehouse we were renting for another of our businesses. The warehouse had a large paved parking lot out back. Once the machine was ready, we needed a test site and the parking lot was an ideal site. We began pouring row after row of freeway barriers, each one demonstrating unresolved bugs in the system. After a year of unsuccessful tinkering, we finally gave up. However, the parking lot was filled with concrete barriers. I occasionally wonder if they are still there.

LESSON 67

Don't buy a concrete extrusion machine to build freeway barriers.

68
DUTCH PLANTERS

One of our ventures was to manufacture light-weight concrete piers to be placed under mobile homes. Traditional piers and jacks were made of steel or solid concrete. Steel prices at the time were sky-rocketing and solid concrete was hard to handle. Our piers came in three sizes, were lightweight and hollow inside for easy stacking and transporting, and had a metal bracket and bolt on the top for leveling the mobile home.

Since concrete has to harden, we produced hundreds of piers and had them curing in a large storage yard.

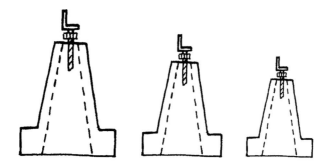

Once we deemed them ready to go, the piers sold quite well.

After the first two weeks of shipping, our telephone began to ring off the hook. Mobile homes were falling to earth as the piers cracked and broke. We immediately went to a testing service and found our design was flawed, but to correct the problem would have raised the price of the piers higher than steel. We were not only out of business, but also had hundreds of pallets of concrete piers to dispose of.

One of our crackerjack salesmen, who was selling our clothing line, said he would take them off our hands at no cost. He jammed a dowel between the big ones and small ones, painted them in bright colors and sold them to Kmart for Dutch planters.

LESSON 68
Concrete can break. Failure can lead to success.

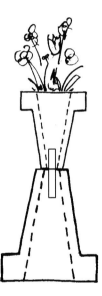

69
BIKE BAGS

One of our, more successful ventures was a clothing and sewing company called *Three Suns Designs*. We bought 51 percent of a growing establishment that was owned by a very creative designer who was designing, manufacturing, and selling from her garage. Products included garden pants, aprons, pillow hats, T–shirts, and bike bags. Once we had our production lines going, we hired a crackerjack salesperson to increase sales. Soon, our bike bag business started to soar.

One of our overall company problems was accounting. It was not unusual that we would be one to three months behind on accounting for any one business. As our bike bag business soared, we eventually discovered our financial losses were also soaring. We discovered our cost of production was higher than our sales price.

LESSON 69
Keep your books up to date.

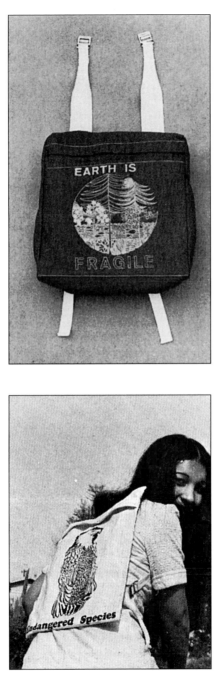

Bike Bags

70
WHISKEY BARRELS

While driving around Fresno one day, our business development officer noticed a large industrial lot stacked high with used whiskey barrels. The owner was a company that reconditioned whiskey barrels. Several national companies were selling furniture made from whiskey barrels, so this looked like a natural venture with a source of barrels right in our backyard.

We built a new furniture factory and soon were in the whiskey barrel furniture business. We only had two problems. First, our workers discovered that if they put a few cups of water in the empty barrels while they sat in the hot Fresno sun, you could extract some pretty fair tasting whiskey. This reduced the productivity of our workforce. And second, while initial sales soared (our salesman was good at getting stores to order one set for the showroom floor) the market for whiskey barrel furniture was very thin and already saturated.

LESSON 70
Just because something hits you in the face, it doesn't make it a good idea.

Whiskey Barrel Arm Chair

Whiskey Barrel Bar

71
FORM YOUR OWN ARMY

One of the advantages—or, in our case, disadvantages—of being a federally funded program was access to surplus government and military equipment through the General Services Administration (GSA). We acquired our own army of old jeeps, trucks, buses, and lots of useless equipment. It was always advisable to obtain more than one of anything for spare parts. Our members used these vehicles and equipment in a variety of ways, with the understanding that if we were ever audited, they would have to bring them in for inspection. Fortunately this never happened or Fresno might have looked like the invasion of Normandy.

I did make one mistake. I needed a Dictaphone, so I had our supply officer bring back six or eight machines. None of these proved to be very workable so I stashed them in the corner of my office. One day, while buying a good Dictaphone from a salesman, he noticed the machines standing in the corner and offered me five dollars apiece in trade. I got my Dictaphone at a discount and cleared my office in one deal. Only later did I remember that I had sold government property.

In many ways, the GSA equipment program was more fun than helpful. I wondered if moving all of this stuff around the country and keeping track of it wasn't costing the government more than it was worth.

I finally put my foot down when some of our members wanted to requisition an airplane or two.

We used to joke that if we couldn't get an economic toehold into the valley any other way, we could move our GSA vehicles into the hills overlooking Interstate 5 and some Sunday swoop down and take over the freeway.

LESSON 71
Sometimes free is expensive.

72
JUST FOR FUN

Moving from the cool climate of the San Francisco Bay Area to the hot Fresno valley lent itself to all sorts of interesting and, in retrospect, funny events.

BEER TIME

One of the businesses our CDC was exploring was a brewery. Since we were primarily a Hispanic corporation, I had in mind a nice, Mexican–tasting beer. Our brewmaster said he could brew any flavor we wanted, since beer is mostly in the marketing. At one of my board of directors meetings, we had a blind beer test to determine which direction we should go. Much to our surprise, the winning beer was Coors, which was, at the time, being boycotted by the labor movement and many Hispanics.

CHASERS

My CDC Hispanic board of directors introduced me to one of the dumbest things I've ever done: drinking Tequila shooters with Wild Turkey chasers. As you might guess, I don't remember much about this, but suffice it to say, I still have an unopened bottle of Wild Turkey sitting in my liquor cabinet, now some 30 years old.

LESSON 72
You can have fun anywhere you live.

73
RIGHT UNDER YOUR NOSE

After I left the community development corporation, my best idea yet finally hit. It would have addressed a series of problems we had.

• We were always trying to reinvent the wheel rather than simply invest in solid, proven businesses.

• We had community organizers in the field but they lacked a base of operation over a very large, 100-by-50-mile project area, located some 20 miles from our office in Fresno.

• Our low-income members always had transportation problems with broken down automobiles and trucks.

• Our low-income members were always looking for places to fix their vehicles.

Within our project area, we had 13 small towns. We could have purchased a gas station in each town, providing a place for our members to buy gas, fix their cars, and have our organizers on site in their offices.

What a great lost idea!

LESSON 73
Sometimes the best ideas are right under your nose.

74
PLANNING'S NOT SO BAD

After five years in economic development, I decided to try my hand again at city planning. Tucson, Arizona, was evidently far enough away from my unsuccessful Marin County, California, political foray that I was hired as Planning Director. It was necessary to downplay the fact that I had graduated from Berkeley, a sore point that some conservatives raised every time they wanted to criticize me.

Having been away from planning for five years, I came back charged up and ready to go. I loved it.

LESSON 74
The planning profession can look better after taking a sabbatical.

PART 8

TUCSON

75
COCKTAIL INTERVIEWS

One of my first duties in Tucson was to hire the very important position of Assistant Planning Director. We flew in six out-of-town candidates for the interviews. Each candidate was put through the paces with multiple interviews, one with me, one with a staff group, one with an official civil service panel, and another with a citizens' panel.

Selecting people for specific positions is always difficult and multiple interviews can be very helpful. However, in this case, we decided to try one more twist to the multiple interview technique. All six candidates were invited to a cocktail reception at my house along with the planning staff, giving us considerable additional insight.

When the city personnel director heard about this, he went ballistic because we violated his view of hiring procedures. But it was too late. The event was over. This is a great idea if you can get away with it.

LESSON 75
Use your creativity in finding ways to provide as much information as possible in the interview process.

76
REDEVELOP YOUR RELATIONSHIPS

I've always felt that planning for redevelopment areas should be done by the planning department, but it seldom is. When I came to Tucson, I saw that the redevelopment staff was housed in a department separate from the planning department. I decided that in order for planning to play a major role, I needed to have a specific plan to develop the relationships between planning and redevelopment.

I went out of my way to assist the redevelopment staff. I also developed personal support for their programs and a relationship with staff that was well-oiled with margaritas at several local hangouts. We soon developed an integral and supportive partnership on redevelopment projects.

LESSON 76

Decide which are your important relationships and develop them through a methodical program.

77
GIVE US YOUR REAL ESTATE

The liberal city council that was in office when I arrived in Tucson was against sprawl, favored inner-city development, and assumed annexation ate up valuable city resources that should be spent on the inner city. While these goals were well intentioned, the annexation policy was a disaster. While I'm not aware of any city or national study that has categorically proved that in the long-term annexation is positive, there are numerous examples of cities that have turned their backs on annexation and now lack the resources to deal with inner-city problems. In Tucson's case, lack of aggressiveness resulted in the creation of three new cities and large areas of unincorporated, developed subdivisions that to this day resist city annexation.

There is an amusing aside to this Tucson story. A former city department head who left the city on less-than-favorable terms became a city manager for one of the new start-up cities. Through his new city's aggressive annexation policy, he managed to snag a new regional shopping center away from Tucson. So much for liberal city policies.

LESSON 77
Annex, annex, annex.

78
GROW SLOW-OR NOT AT ALL

When I arrived in Tucson, there was a heated debate underway about growth. Should the community encourage growth, discourage growth, or remain relatively neutral? There were several strong staff advocates for discouraging growth, as well as a few elected officials at both the city and county levels suggesting discouraging growth or perhaps even favoring no growth.

It is clear that a small community or subarea of a larger community can find mechanisms to limit growth, but to attempt that for an entire region like Tucson is another matter. Our economic consultants told us that growth was heavily impacted by regional migration patterns and the overall national and state economy, neither of which local government had much control over. Because the debate was so hot, I challenged the staff planners who favored no or slow growth to write an alternative to the General Plan for the community to consider. Features of this alternative included:

• Zoning ordinance would be reviewed and revised to reflect the desired maximum rates of growth.

• New growth should pay its own way.

• Firms adding 100 or more employees must file a growth impact statement and may be denied, delayed, or scaled down.

• Recruitment of industrial commercial firms and promotion and advertising of tourism would become the full responsibility of the private sector.

• If the above doesn't work, firms with 50 or more employees must follow growth impact statements; federal, state, and university agencies would be requested to cancel or delay expansion plans; and quotas for new residential building permits shall be established.

The city and county chose not to adopt these recommendations. Even entering this debate seemed to reflect negatively on the planning department. Since then, I've become convinced that virtually all elected officials will support economic development activities irrespective of their stance on growth. From a regional perspective, this debate is not worth entering.

I did postulate once that if a community lets its infrastructure go to pot, has poor schools, little environmental protection, and poor job creation, the rate of growth will slow or even become negative, i.e. many of our central cities. But is this acceptable public policy?

LESSON 78
Government attempts at slow growth or no growth on a regional basis are not likely to be successful. Planners, let this sleeping dog lie.

79
ROUND TABLES

During the heat of the battle on the comprehensive plan, we decided to try another technique. We advertised a hearing by the staff to receive testimony on the plan. Several of us sat up front at a table similar to the way a planning commission would function and we received testimony from both supporters and opponents. In concept, this might have been useful. However, those of us sitting up front chose to ask many questions of the speakers and in some cases adopted what may have seemed like an interrogation of the presenters. Perhaps elected or appointed officials can get away with this but staff can't. All we had accomplished through this effort was to further alienate those who were already against the plan.

As our relationship with the opponents got worse and worse, we tried another approach. I met with three or four of the strong and influential opponents in a series of private meetings. We sat around a round table as equals, began to understand each others' positions, and arrived at useful compromise language and policy.

LESSON 79
Use a round table and, as a planner, recognize that you do not sit at the head of the table.

80
MAKE LITTLE PLANS

The draft Tucson Comprehensive Plan was 561 pages long and just under two inches thick. I see similar plan documents throughout the country. It's virtually impossible for policy makers, citizens, and even staff to comprehend and use such large documents. As a first cut in Tucson, we edited this plan down to a half-inch document consisting of 103 pages of background material and 50 pages of policy. Had the community decided to proceed with this plan further, I'm certain it could have been reduced once again, perhaps to half this size.

LESSON 80
Make little plans, people may actually understand them.

81
WHY NOT DESIGN?

The draft Comprehensive Plan was heavily orient-ed toward growth control and socioeconomic issues. While many of the issues were sound and sup-ported by a majority of the liberal city council, the panel was soon recalled (see Chapter 87) and replaced by a conservative council. We continued to plow ahead with community meetings and plan hearings on a lost cause. In retrospect, we should have tabled this work to a more appropriate time. In fact, that time did arrive a number of years after I left Tucson.

One of the plan's key opponents was active in the Urban Land Institute and a supporter of design issues. In retrospect we could have and should have shifted to design issues, landscape, Southwest architecture, mountain views, corridors, billboards, commercial revitalization, and the like. I believe at that point in time all of these would have had a much more recep-tive audience.

LESSON 81
Timing is important in planning. Have a variety of projects and strategies ready. Match them to the political climate of the time.

82
RENT-A-LAWN

Migration to Tucson was heavy from the Midwest, where people pride themselves on expansive green lawns. While lawns like those are totally inappropriate for a desert environment, one of the first things most Midwesterners did after moving to Tucson was to have a nursery remove the desert landscape and plant grass.

However, after two or three years of the Midwesterners acclimating to the desert, the nursery would be called to replace the lawn with desert plants. The local nurseries undoubtedly made a lot of money from this routine.

As a public policy, I thought we should require a three-year waiting period for new residents before they would be allowed to plant grass, similar to the waiting period for buying a gun. In practice, we began to restrict the growing of grass in new subdivisions and raised water prices to discourage the growing of grass.

LESSON 82
Think twice before planting grass; learn to acclimate to your local environment.

83
DRY RIVERS

In many communities, rivers can form an ecological and psychological focus for the community, yet they are often ignored or hidden. In Tucson, we decided to take a comprehensive approach to the 14 miles of the Santa Cruz River that bisects the city by creating a river master plan. Arizona rivers are unique in that for many months they are dry. This requires citizens to see them in a new light.

The Santa Cruz River Master Plan was described as:

"A series of events proposed to take place in and along the Santa Cruz River in its 14-mile course through the City of Tucson. The plan itself is, for the most part, concerned with the physical aspects of the river and its environment—improvement of the river channel, developing a water management system and building the park, roads and other public facilities.

"The physical improvements will solve certain problems and will also have significant value in themselves. The improved river channel will accommodate the 100-year flood and will increase groundwater recharge. The park along the reshaped banks will make it possible to recycle sewage effluent, increase linkages to other community elements, improve wildlife habitat and enhance the environment of adjacent lands. Roads, visitor centers and adjacent parks will offer other opportunities for cultural and leisure-time activities and allow movement among neighborhoods and the various elements of the riverpark system.

"The physical plan, the scholarly and technological systems and the free play of social, cultural and economic forces all become interrelated in the single concept of the riverpark. The master plan, which develops this concept, does so in firm and precise statements."

This was a bold plan, likely requiring 50 or more years for its implementation. Moshe Safdie, creator of Habitat at the Canadian World's Fair, once observed that big, bold ideas often require a single person with commitment and vision to stick with the plan for many years. I left Tucson shortly after the plan was adopted. The County Flood Control District, an organization with substantial resources and commitment, agreed to take a leadership role in implementing the plan. Now, some 20 years later, the plan and its implementation are well under way. Furthermore, the concept is accepted as a given in the community and has been expanded to some 100 linear miles of river corridors.

SANTA CRUZ RIVERPARK
CITY OF TUCSON, ARIZONA

LESSON 83
Big plans need a sponsor. It's even better if the sponsor has deep pockets.

84
SEX

In the mid-1970s, two female planners from the San Francisco Bay Area became concerned about negative aspects of sexual imagery and other women's issues. They put together a two-screen slide show and lecture series and agreed to present it for my department in Tucson at no charge if I paid their expenses.

I arranged a meeting room outside City Hall and had a number of local women's organizations cosponsor the event. At the last minute, we had a problem with our meeting room and had to move our presentation to the City Hall council chambers. Included in the show were six or eight slides of male and female nudes that were used to make various points. I remember seeing a male nude taken from *Playgirl* magazine on the left screen and the Washington Monument on the right screen.

The next day, headlines in the Tucson newspapers read, "Zucker Puts on Sex Show in City Hall."

The mayor, who wanted to see my head on a platter in any case, immediately took up the charge. The cosponsoring women's groups took up the defense and the war of words was on. Several letters to the mayor suggested he was probably just angry because he wasn't as well endowed as the male model in the slideshow. As the events became more and more heated, it became clear that this was a no-win situation. Eventually, everyone backed off.

I kept my job and the next week received a dozen red roses from the two speakers.

LESSON 84
Get a cosponsor for your politically controversial events.

85
IDEAS STICK

In one of my 1998 planning seminars, I had an attendee, Karen Dotson, who worked for me in Tucson in 1976. She indicated she still followed some philosophical nuggets I had written in 1976 which I had long since lost. She sent me a copy which read:

1. Today vs. 2000
Planning is the act of making short-term recommendations based on an understanding of long-term impact and projections. It is not planning for the year 2000: it is effecting today's action.

2. Exploring the Options—Understanding Other Perspectives
Ours is a pluralistic society that at times must work in unison. Your role is to understand all sides of a debate or conflict. To explore options, to present facts. Finally, to take a position and make a judgment that is based on proper understanding and research. It is most important to communicate and continue to communicate with those who may have a different position than you. Try to understand that position better than the person who holds it. It will either change your mind, or at least sharpen your position and check your accuracy.

We can also do this for each other. That's why open debate and disagreement are so important. Open your mouth and also your mind (not always in that order).

No staff member is hired to agree with any other staff member, including the Director. Honest, intelligent debate is not only acceptable, but demanded of all staff members. Staff members who are not handling a project, but who have constructive criticisms, are encouraged to submit them for the benefit of staff analysis.

3. Ideas

We must proceed on the assumption that we cannot achieve our goals if we maintain our traditional methods. The old answers will not do. Planners have been doing the same things for years simply because all the other planners have been doing the same things the same old ways. Tucson is not just one of thousands of cities. It is not just a political subdivision of the State of Arizona. Tucson is unique in geography, history, and the works of man. The Planning Department must match this uniqueness. A staff whose performance, procedures, and programs are "up to date" may just not be good enough for Tucson. We must lead—not merely follow the blind. So think! Reason! This is what you're getting paid for. Ideas please!

Although a lot has changed in 20-some years, I still like these plannerese ideas.

LESSON 85
Don't be afraid to expound your philosophy—it just may stick.

86
WRONG NUMBER

It was well known in Tucson that the mayor and I didn't see eye to eye on many issues. The following article appeared in the July 3, 1975, issue of the *St. Petersburg Times*.

He Got The Wrong Zucker

A University of Arizona student says he didn't have the heart to tell Mayor Lew Murphy of Tucson that he was talking to the wrong man Tuesday night. Paul S. Zucker said he received a telephone call from someone who said, "Lew Murphy here," and then launched into 10 minutes of praise for remarks on city planning he thought Zucker made on a local television show Monday night. Apparently, Mayor Murphy meant to call Paul C. Zucker. The student said he hung up the telephone without telling the mayor he had the wrong man. "I just said 'thank you' three or four times and then 'goodbye,'" he said.

After seeing the article, I waited for the mayor to call. I'm still waiting.

LESSON 86
Sometimes you do good and don't know it.

87
WATER WARS

When I ran for the Board of Supervisors in Marin County, I tried to find a single issue to excite the electorate, but with no success. Politicians in Tucson had no such problem.

When I arrived, the City of Tucson had a liberal City Council (three to two) with the courage to tackle important issues. One of these issues was water. Tucson existed solely on groundwater wells, and for many years, the groundwater table had been dropping by 10 to 15 feet per year. It was clear that the city would eventually run out of water, the only question was when.

In order to address this issue, the City Council adopted a progressive water rate plan that essentially tripled water fees for many users. As might be expected, all hell broke loose. The first successful recall in the history of Arizona took place. Overnight, it went from perhaps the most liberal council in the history of the city to the most conservative—which immediately lowered the water rates.

A few years later, the water rates were back where the liberals had set them. The new council raised them a small amount each year.

LESSON 87
Sometimes incrementalism is the best approach.

88
LUNCH WITH YOUR ENEMY

As one might expect, the new conservative members of the City Council had no time for or inclination toward planning. One of the new council members immediately called for the planning director (me) to be fired.

As a gesture of a good will, I invited this councilor to lunch. He accepted and I made reservations at a restaurant that I knew was frequented by politicians, city hall insiders, and city activists. Seeing the two of us at lunch created an interesting stir among those folks and, I believe, had the desired effect of putting off the firing squad.

LESSON 88
Keep your olive branch handy.

89
MOVE IT

When I arrived in Tucson, the city had the most liberal City Council in its history. Following the water wars and the City Council recall, the city had its most conservative council in its history. During this two-year span, we were trying to adopt a new comprehensive plan.

This kind of situation can age a planning director very fast, so I decided to move on to San Diego County as an Assistant County Administrator in charge of an organization called the Integrated Planning Office (IPO).

LESSON 89
Know when to move on.

PART 9

SAN DIEGO

90
WHO ARE THE PLANNERS?

The newspapers in both Tucson and San Diego described my move to San Diego as going from the "frying pan into the fire." For once, the newspapers were right. The Integrated Planning Office (IPO) was the brainchild of an elected official who decided it would be great to put all the planners in the county into one organization. Each county department identified its planners and sent them on to the new organization. This had numerous problems.

One, in separating the land-use planners doing long-range planning from those processing entitlements and permitting created a massive communication problem.

Two, it assumed that operating departments didn't need to do any planning—it could all be done elsewhere.

Three, it appeared that many departments "cooked the books" to identify their least productive people and label them as planners so they could be transferred out. Or, it's possible the planners were in fact their least productive people.

After a few years of this, at my suggestion, IPO was disbanded.

LESSON 90
Keep long- and short-range land-use planners together, and also recognize that operating departments need to be concerned about planning.

91
ENGINEERS AND PLANNERS-OIL AND WATER?

The Integrated Planning Office's purpose was to coordinate the planning related to the physical development of the county in the area of transportation, land use, sanitation, environmental management, and capital facilities. In addition to merging all the planners from various departments the merger also included many engineers.

One county employee, Michael McNamara—in partial fulfillment of his Master of Business Administration at Pepperdine University—prepared a research project to examine the existence of professional stereotypes between engineers and planners. McNamara postulated as follows:

"The two disciplines that were studied represent two different cultural systems. The engineers come from a profession that has been established in some form or another for more than 100 years. Planners come from a profession in which one-half of the professional programs came into being within the past fifteen years. The engineer operates in a world where facts can be measured and the outcome is within prescribed boundaries that all engineers can analyze, test, and agree upon. The planners operate in a world where decisions are based on value judgments or upon political considerations. The engineers come from a scientific background which demands a great deal of discipline and methodical study for mastery. Planners come

from a social science background which tends to be related to the helping professions. There is evidence of a split between the people-oriented helping professions such as planning and the object-oriented professions such as engineering. The people workers tend to be resentful of the object manipulators and take pains to avoid being identified with them."

So what did McNamara find?

"The interesting conclusion of this research project is that the suspected stereotypes were not. Engineers and planners did not hold stereotypes about each other that could be demonstrated to be statistically significant.

"As a general conclusion, it may be stated that stereotypes between engineers and planners have not been demonstrated to be a problem which affects the interaction of interdisciplinary groups. It was probably best said by an anonymous respondent from the IPO who said that 'of all the problems in IPO, that relationship is not one of them.'"

It's interesting to place this research in a contemporary context. While once rare, I see more and more communities across the country merging engineers and planners who work on the development process into one, integrated department. The stereotype that many once thought inhibited this merger, may in fact, not exist.[†]

LESSON 91
Engineers and planners can row in the same boat.

[†]One of the reviewers for this book was one of my key assistants in IPO, Rick Morey. He was less sanguine about how well the planners and engineers in fact got along. Planners and engineers do approach the world from a different perspective, but these differences can add strength to an organization.

92
OFFICE NIGHTMARES

The County Planning Department of San Diego was located in the historic San Diego County Civic Center located on picturesque San Diego Bay. The offices had a view of the bay and downtown. During lunch we could walk along the water, eating fish and chips or walk to a nearby Little Italy for lunch. The Board of Supervisors wanted to develop a one-stop shop for building, planning, health, and engineering permits, but there was no room for all these functions in the Civic Center. A number of years earlier, the county had purchased a 300,000-square-foot concrete tiltup warehouse. The building was gradually being used for overflow offices. The "offices"—and I use that term loosely—had nine-foot drop ceilings, power poles to bring electricity down from above, and no windows. They were terrible; an inhuman environment. This was the selected site to put together a 100,000-square-foot permit center.

I fought this project long and hard. Eventually the County Administrator told me the train was leaving the station. It was time for me to get on board or get off.

Having lost the battle, I was determined to improve on what had been done in the past. I was added to the architectural selection committee and we managed to veto all but one architect, the only one who showed any concern for the inhuman aspects of the building. We worked closely with that architect to create a high-ceiling central courtyard with skylights and trees, several miniparks with benches, three to four different ceiling heights, playful wall dividers, and designs and tile pathways. The General Services Department, which was in charge of the remodel, fought us every step of the way.

When the construction was finished, it was deemed magnificent and received several awards. The *Los Angeles Times* asked for a tour and wrote a glowing article on the remodel. The General Services Director, who had fought the designs, led the tour and carefully explained "his" grand concepts.

Although we would have preferred the waterfront, this was not a bad second choice.

LESSON 92
You can create a silk purse from a sow's ear.

Remodeled Warehouse

Ugly warehouse becomes a 'Taj Mahal'

By Reggie Smith
Tribune Staff Writer

When the county bought a warehouse five years ago, the building was quickly dubbed "a white elephant."

Although the structure had a tendency to leak badly at the first sign of rain, many county officials thought the ugly barn-like building on Ruffin Road in Kearny Mesa was a steal at $3 million.

Now it is undergoing a $2.5 million remodeling that has prompted some county staff members to give it a new nickname: Taj Mahal.

"If it doesn't cost any more to become a Taj Mahal, why shouldn't we?" asked Paul Zucker, the county's planning chief, who is behind renovating the northwest section of the building to house the county's permit-processing staff in July.

Zucker says he doesn't think that what he is doing with the county's annex operations center comes close to being grandiose, that he's just trying to make working in the 340,000-square-foot tomb more tolerable.

He admits that workers in more conventionally attired offices in the annex are a bit envious.

The 22-foot-high ceilings will have skylights, full-sized trees will grow from holes in the cement floor, and walls will be brightly colored.

Zucker got the architect to vary the height of the ceilings from 10 to 22 feet.

Plans show large sections where the skylight, trees and a few branches give that "feeing of being outdoors," he said. The cost of the renovation has its critics.

Supervisor Roger Hedgecock first called the Ruffin Road annex a "white elephant" after his election in 1977.

Hedgecock said yesterday that he voted to approve the move because he wanted to make it more convenient for people seeking approval of construction permits to go through the maze of county departments.

But $2.5 million?

"That's too much," said Hedgecock. "Everything we do around here is too much."

Zucker's present office is on the bay front at the County Center on PacificHighway downtown.

As part of a two-year plan for a one-stop center for processing construction permits and other permits, the county is moving all the functions of its Planning Department and related departments under one roof.

That roof happens to be the Ruffin Road annex, where some county departments, including the registrar of voters are. But, for the most part, the massive structure is now used as an expensive storage space.

"It's not Taj Mahal," said Bob King, acting assistant director of general services."It doesn't have the nice window with a bay view like the downtown building has, but I think they are trying to make a barn as livable as possible, from an office standpoint."

This is why Zucker has been in on the remodeling work from the start.

"He's demanded and got, from what I understand, a first-class operation,"said Chief Administrator Clifford Graves.

"He's not spending any more money, but he's taken a personal interest in seeing that the place looks nice.

"He feels, as I do, that employees work better in pleasant environments."

93
LAY OFF THE LAYOFFS

In the San Diego County planning program, we were rapidly moving to a full cost-recovery budget based on fees. This worked well during the boom development days, but created major headaches during the 1980 and 1981 building recession. In the first year of that recession alone, we ran a $1.5 million deficit that had to be absorbed by the general fund. As would be natural, as the department's director, I was accused of creating this deficit even though the elected officials refused to close field offices and take other precipitous actions we proposed to bring the deficit down.

Finally, we were faced with the dreaded word—layoff. The County Civil Service System was structured on a seniority basis, meaning last hire in was the first one out. This meant we were about to lay off some of our newest and brightest stars. To counter this, we researched the rules and used every possible nuance of the civil service policies to achieve as many selective layoffs as possible.

The Civil Service Board overturned most of our manipulation and in the process, we created major turmoil within the department. Layoffs at best are difficult. Manipulating the system can make it even worse. Don't try to correct your lack of effort to deal with poor performers through a layoff system.

LESSON 93
If faced with layoffs, use clear rules, not manipulation.

94
SAVE IT FOR LATER

San Diego has lost count of the number of studies completed to find a site to relocate the constrained one-runway city airport—Lindbergh Field.

The County Planning Department was involved in one of these studies and thought the Miramar Naval Air Station would one day be available as a relocation site. It was an excellent location already configured as an airport, only some 15 to 20 minutes from downtown. Since San Diego long has been a military town and the Top Gun forces were located at Miramar, the possibility of the military powers abandoning this facility was not a politically great idea. But like many political debates, the issue was treated like the region was designing a house rather than working on a long-term solution to its airport problems. The military indicated they had no intention of abandoning Miramar. The elected officials, living in a military town, didn't want to rock the boat or pressure the military.

Lacking political support, we made another recommendation. Don't agree to move the airport to Miramar, but do adopt land-use policies aimed at preserving Miramar as a long-term airport option. We had some mild political support for this approach and some surrounding land-use categories were changed in response.

Twenty years later, as part of the national effort to close military establishments and realign facilities, Top Gun and its sibling were indeed moved out of

Miramar. This created an ideal time to again approach the military to abandon Miramar, but still the politicians dawdled. Instead, the Marines moved in with their noisy helicopters.

I firmly believe the idea will rise again, probably in the next round of base closings. Let's hope for some political will at that time. In the meantime, the contingency land-use changes may yet protect this facility for future commercial use.

LESSON 94
Keep contingency planning in your bag of tricks.

95
MORE FLAMES

Through the years, I've not only been fired, but I've had the job of firing numerous employees. This task is never easy, but is part of the manager's responsibility.

Employees are not fired because they are bad people. They are fired because they are the wrong person in that environment and with the others they work or associate with. Helping your employees to find their best job or job fit is a gift to them. You do not do them a favor by accepting poor performance or a poor job fit.

Many of the people I've fired are still good friends today. They have thanked me for helping them find the right fit. I'm writing this chapter as part of the San Diego section because that experience gave me good examples of this theory. It also reminded me of some earlier experiences. Successful transitions included:

Wrong Position	Right Position
Assistant Director	Director
Junior Planner	Park Ranger
Assistant Planner	Landscape Architect
Senior Planner	College Professor

LESSON 95
Help your staff find their most productive positions.

96
PAY ME NOW AND PAY ME LATER

Once we moved toward full cost-recovery for services, it occurred to us that some of our fees weren't high enough to cover complex development projects. To compensate, we converted many of our fixed fee schedules to variable fees and put in a consulting type fee program based on actual costs.

While at first this worked well, it was fraught with problems. First it required a complex timekeeping and billing system. When we had a high volume workload, fees tended to be low because staff was spread thin and worked quite efficiently. However, in a time of low workload, staff felt it had to put their time somewhere so recorded it against projects. After I left the county and began to process projects for developers, it was not unusual for the county to charge more to review a project than we were charging our clients in the first place, to design the project.

While this system might be good in theory, many planning or community development departments are not capable of managing staff to adequately run such a system. As such, the system tends to run amok.

LESSON 96
Fixed fees aren't so bad after all.

97
TIME WAITS FOR EVERYONE

In many respects, the San Diego County General Plan was a disaster. It was one of those two-volume, six-inch-thick documents that was hard to use and comprehend. However, many of its policies had been developed under more planning-progressive elected officials than we now found as our leaders. Should we launch a redo or let sleeping dogs lie? We let them lie.

Through the years, I've noted that antiplanning elected officials will continue the more progressive planning policies of their predecessors through inaction, inertia, or complacency.

LESSON 97

Use timing as part of your planning strategy.

98
FORMER FRIENDLY FARMERS

My success with agricultural preservation in Marin County (see Chapter 47) may have led me to be a bit too casual or even cocky with our developing an agricultural plan and strategy for San Diego County. We completed many of the plannerese standard things. We mapped all the soils by type; we had economists examine the economics of agricultural production; we created a plan to protect the best agricultural land from urbanization. We were then soundly defeated at the political level. What went wrong?

As is often the case, we will never know for certain what happened. In retrospect, it seems to me that:

- The amount of prime agricultural land in San Diego County is relatively limited.

- The timelines between future urbanization and agricultural land was relatively short. Another way to say this is the land's speculative value was very high compared with its agricultural value.

- San Diego had more land speculators than true farmers.

Given the political environment, I'm not certain that any proposal could have been adopted. However, I speculate that some form of transfer of development rights would have fared better.

LESSON 98
Agricultural preservation will work best when plans are many years ahead of the land speculation curve.

99
LET'S TALK

I once belonged to what I considered to be one of the world's worst organizations, the California County Planning Directors Association. It wasn't that the members weren't intelligent and good drinking buddies, it was just that those of us planners for urban counties like San Diego had little in common with the small rural counties, kindly referred to as "cow counties."

To fill a void, I suggested to the Southern California urban counties—Orange, Los Angeles, San Bernardino, Riverside and Ventura—that we directors meet once a month to see what we could learn from each other. It would be just the directors, no staff. My peer directors thought it was a great idea and I agreed to host the first session.

I spent a lot of time putting together a one-inch-thick notebook describing our San Diego program and we spent a delightful day talking about it. Everyone claimed it was extremely useful. However, this was the first and last meeting of the group. I could never get another one of the directors to organize the next session.

One good thing did come out of this effort. I used my notebook along with a few other ideas to write my first book, *The Management Idea Book*, that sold out its first two printings.

LESSON 99
We can learn from each other, but not without talking.

100
WHAT YOU SEE IS WHAT YOU SEE

For years I've been fascinated by the ideas expressed in a 1955 British book called *Outrage/Counter Attack*. The idea was to divide England into five types of areas: wild, country, arcadia (subdivision by our terminology), town, and metropolis. The design theme for each would be consistent with that area. The publication included examples for seats, footpads, railings, walls and hedges, street furniture, lettering, paint, shelters, utilities, building lines, site lines, monuments, trees, advertising, street lighting, parks, ornamental planting, wires, industry, military installations, roads, and parking lots.

I've often thought of this study when helping some communities to define their desired image. It's not unusual to find people living in relatively high density areas wanting to think of themselves as rural. One way to reinforce a rural image would be to put those places where we spend so much time (major highways) into rural corridors. We once began to study this idea for San Diego County. The idea was to require development along three of our major freeway corridors to be clustered so as not to be visible from the freeway. We did study this for a while but didn't have the fortitude to push it in to the public debate. Another big idea that didn't make it.

LESSON 100

Rural is what rural seems.

101
MAKE NO LITTLE PLANS

Looking back over my 40 years in planning, I like to say I never got in trouble for my big ideas, only the little ones. I never regretted the big ideas I surfaced, only the big ideas I didn't think of, or the ones I didn't suggest.

Looking back at my five years as a San Diego County Assistant County Administrator for Planning, I often think of how we missed some big ideas. Every year, our management team went on an overnight retreat to the mountains or desert to regroup. During many of these retreats we tried to have a session on the "big ideas." What were we missing? What should planning really be addressing? Where was the county going? In retrospect, we came up dry. In many aspects this was not just a reflection on us, but rather a reflection on where planning seems to have arrived. I started my career in Philadelphia and Boston watching the Two Eds with the big ideas (Ed Bacon, Philadelphia Planning Director, and Ed Logue, Boston Redevelopment Director). Where have the Eds gone?

Some 20 years later, thanks to hindsight, only a few big ideas for San Diego have surfaced. Some undoubtedly are still underground.

  • San Diego City and County have created one of the country's first and largest multispecies habitat conservation programs, covering some 580,000 acres of the region. Not only will this preserve habitat and large areas of open space, but also allow development to proceed outside protected boundaries.

• Work is under way to create an ocean-to-mountains San Diego River Valley park, potentially encompassing a 55-mile-long corridor.

• Other big ideas have been discussed for years, but may never be achieved, such as linking San Diego Bay to Mission Bay by an inland waterway and linking the famous Balboa Park to San Diego Bay.

I once dreamed of studying why our citizens are so alienated from government and how our planning adds to or detracts from the socialization of people— a high-touch topic in a high-tech era. One more big idea that got away.

As a crowning "little plan debate," perhaps nowhere in the United States is a better big idea opportunity being lost than in San Diego. The 500-acre, soon-to-be-reused San Diego Naval Training Center could be combined with the outdated 500-acre San Diego Airport (which could easily be moved to a military base no longer used by Top Gun) and 50 acres of adjacent industrial land vacated by a former military contractor. All have bay and ocean access within minutes of downtown San Diego. The result could be developed into one of the world's grandest in-town, multi-use, water-oriented communities (including the Bay–to–Bay link)—the Venice of the West Coast. Instead, the city is going to get a few more parking spaces for airplanes, a fire training facility, parking for rental car companies, 500 units of military housing, maybe a hotel and some odds and ends. My, my— make small plans. Where is Daniel Burnham when we need him?

LESSON 101
Big ideas are out there. Planners need to find and sell them.

102
ALL THE NEWS THAT'S FIT TO PRINT

In order to communicate with a planning staff of 300-plus, I created a weekly 10- to 20-page newsletter called the *Plutonic.*

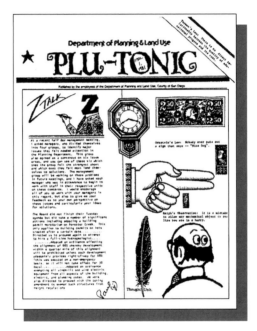

The publication worked because everyone contributed articles, none of which was edited. The *Plutonic* became so popular that people outside the department often asked for copies. One of our cartoons did get us in trouble, as discussed in the newspaper article.

LESSON 102
Sometimes all the news that's fit to print isn't.

Risque country newsletter prompts scrutiny

By Reggie Smith
Tribune Staff Writer

The first frame of the cartoon shows Napoleon on horseback as he peers down at a woman sleeping alone in a double bed.

The second frame—the punch line—shows the woman and the horse cuddled together in the bed while the famed French emperor looks on dejectedly.

It's not the kind of material usually found in stodgy bureaucratic newsletters.

But then, the "PLU-TONIC" is not your average in-house newsletter.

It is, in fact, the brainchild of Paul Zucker, the county's Planning and Land Use Department director, who actively encourages the PLU-TONIC's attempts at humor.

In hindsight, however, Zucker admits he probably wouldn't have allowed the cartoon to run in the weekly newsletter had he seen it beforehand.

"Some people thought it was sexist," he says.

And one of those people apparently is county Supervisor Tom Hamilton, who said he's received complaints from Zucker's staff about the content of the newsletter and the time it takes to put the thing together.

After reviewing the latest edition, which included the Napoleon comic strip, Hamilton said, "I believe it is an inappropriate publication and an unnecessary expenditure of public funds.

"In my opinion, any relevant information can be disseminated to employees through standard department memos without the need for jokes and social commentaries."

Hamilton asked Ruben Dominguez, assistant chief administrator, to look into the matter.

Zucker, on the other hand, says the newsletter makes sense.

"I'm trying to build morale and allow people to have a good time," he said, noting that the PLU-TONIC is not edited by him, nor does he see many of the items before they get into print.

"It's clear government employees are a bit demoralized," said Zucker. "The public's down on them, and they need reinforcement. The letter is a combination of trying to communicate important things and build the workers' morale."

Zucker said the costs are minimal, amounting to three hours of paste-up work by two office staffers and the cost of making about 300 photocopies.

"I partially agree that there needs to be a balance" between news and comedy," he said.

"But it's very important to keep this think free and on a non-edited basis. Everything goes in unless it's obviously too offensive or goes overboard in the political arena, like if someone said a certain supervisor was an s.o.b. I would hope that that wouldn't go in."

183

103
KIDS, KIDS, KIDS

Although the need for day care is a hot topic in the '90s, it was also a major concern in the '80s. Some of my staff, led by Administrative Manager Rick Morey, decided to face the problem head-on and create a day care center right on our office parking lot. Through much hard work and politicking, they obtained two unused portable offices and a budget of $50,000 from the county to create a day care center handling 53 children.

A dissenting vote by one County Supervisor likened the use of county funds for the facility to "socialism in Russia."

LESSON 103
If you're going to be likened to socialism, make it for a good cause.

CHILD CARE CENTER

SAN DIEGO COUNTY EMPLOYEES

County Day Care Center

104
LOSING FAITH

The average tenure of San Diego County Planning Directors before I was hired had been two years. After five years on the job, it became clear that my effectiveness had also passed, and I resigned.

My five years had been a rocky road, but occasionally lightened by newspaper articles like the one below.

The Political Compliment

As San Diego County's planning director, Paul Zucker does not have a smooth sail. He is criticized frequently by one member or another of the Board of Supervisors over county growth plans.

No one has yet devised a way to please all five supervisors on that one.

But the other day Zucker received something of a compliment from Supervisor Jim Bates, who called one of his reports the work of a "competent bureaucrat."

Shaken by those more-or-less kind words, Zucker said later, "I'm starting to lose faith in myself."

—JACK JONES

LESSON 104

Don't let praise go to your head.

PART 10

CONSULTING

105
SO YOU WANT TO BE A MANAGEMENT CONSULTANT?

After leaving my job as San Diego County Planning Director, I wrote *The Management Idea Book* and presented these ideas in a four-carousel slide show at the Dallas national APA conference. An Assistant City Manager from a medium-sized city happened to attend my session. A few weeks later he called me and asked me to conduct a study of his city's planning department for a nice fee.

I said yes, hung up the telephone, and said to myself, "How does one audit a planning department?" In desperation, I called two of my former department administrators and invited them to lunch. The topic was: What does Paul do next?

This task was a sink-or-swim experience. Fortunately, I swam. The city was pleased, and it launched a new career for me as an organizational and management consultant.

LESSON 105
When opportunity knocks, get your feet wet and learn to swim.

106
TREES AND CARS

Most engineers prefer to site trees as far away from the roadway as possible. Generally, it's only the old streets where the trees are next to the curb; in most cities the sidewalk is often next to the curb in newer areas. In one of my consulting jobs, I worked with a city that actually placed the trees in the street. This was a downtown area with angle parking, where the trees were planted between the parking spaces. Of course, occasionally one would get hit by a car or need to be replaced, but what a delightful street scene.

Trees in the Street

Today with the traffic calming ideas, we're seeing a few cities return the trees to the middle of the street.

Tree in Middle of Street

Hanging in my office is an original Richard Hedman cartoon that took this concept even further.

LESSON 106
Put the trees where they belong ... in the street.

Richard Hedman Cartoon

107
FIRE

I was once approached by a city that had just spent $100,000 for a planning consultant to prepare a new general plan. Not producing what the city wanted, the planning consultant was fired. This community was notorious as an impossible place to work, with raucous politics that swung wildly and a split city council.

Given the politics, my firm decided the only way to take on this project was with one provision: The city council and planning commission were to meet in joint session one Saturday a month until the effort was complete. Nine months of meeting in this fashion produced a unanimous plan adoption that included downzoning one-third of the city.

LESSON 107
Find the proper structure to help the policy makers do their job.

108
CERTIFIABLY LIMITED PLANNERS

The California Environmental Quality Act (CEQA) came into existence in 1970. The act requires discretionary actions be examined for possible environmental impact. Many states have since followed with similar legislation.

CEQA has hatched a whole new profession, quite apart from the planning profession: the Association of Environmental Professionals (AEP). Some communities have separate planning and environmental departments or divisions. Many planners no longer see environmental issues as within their domain. Many communities require that only "approved environmentalists," not planners, can prepare environmental analysis. When I left San Diego County, I was not certified to prepare environmental documents even though I created many of the environmental policies and had managed the environmental staff.

In our management and organizational consulting practice, we always recommend merging environmental and planning divisions and retraining the planners to also be environmentalists.

LESSON 108
Policemen must know the laws; planners should know the environment.

109
GIVE ME MORE COMPLAINTS

Most customers who have a problem with an organization are reluctant to complain. In fact, national statistics show that only four percent complain—the other 96 percent remain angry and tell nine or 10 other people. Developers are particularly reluctant to complain to planning or building departments for fear of retribution.

I was given a major lesson in this phenomenon by one of our clients. Every six months, the City Council and staff had monthly meetings with the development community to hear about complaints and work on reform. Before implementing the recommendations, I was asked to test these ideas with developer focus groups. Much to everyone's surprise, a third of the proposed recommendations were unpopular with the group and the most important recommendations had never even surfaced during the monthly meetings. The focus groups were willing to share their complaints with me, an impartial outsider, but not directly with the city.

How can an organization improve? By listening to its customers and finding ways to get them to air their complaints.

LESSON 109
View complaints about your organization as a precious gift—they aren't easy to come by.

110
UP TO MY NECK IN ALLIGATORS

I was hired by a mayor who wanted to improve his city's development process. After a brief review, it was clear that the process was broken and had been broken for 10 or more years. Developers even indicated that they no longer wished to build in the city. Everyone I interviewed, city staff and developers, felt I was wasting my time. Although the mayor talked about the problems, he was unwilling to take the actions necessary to solve them.

I characterized the situation this way: The mayor would stick his head out of his office and shout down the hall, "If you departments were only more efficient, we wouldn't have these problems." The department heads would shout back, "We're so deep in alligators that we can't think about efficiency." They were both right.

The mayor had an absolute policy aversion to hiring more staff. I accepted this as a given and then proposed the interim use of consultants to give the departments time to right their ships. The logjam was broken.

LESSON 110
Every problem has a solution, no matter how elusive it may seem. Be the one to find it.

111
LET'S MAKE A DEAL

I was hired as part of a team to plan the outskirts of a large, rapidly growing city. The contract was with the city, but much of the 150-square-mile planning area was in the unincorporated county. Three large corporations owned most of the unincorporated land area.

Our team did the usual planning things, such as looking at environmental and infrastructure factors, setting forth new town and new urbanization concepts, and the like. However, we missed the major point. Unless the property owners decided to annex, our plan had no validity or chance of implementation. The county was happy to go its own way and ignore our great plan.

A better approach would have been for the mayor to approach the three corporations and cut an annexation deal. Then we would have been in a position to do some real planning.

LESSON 111
Sometimes it's necessary to cut a deal before the real planning can begin.

112
GENERAL MOTORS IN 1950

A Maryland county asked me to conduct a series of training sessions and retreats for the planning staff. When I arrived, I discovered what may be one of the best planning programs in the country. However, the planners were arrogant and resistant to change. They knew they were good and felt they had seen it all.

I found it impossible to penetrate this group until a new thought crossed my mind. I told them they reminded me of General Motors in the '50s. The question was, would they become the General Motors of the '90s. This image finally opened the door to our communications.

LESSON 112
Focusing on continuous improvement is essential for organizational vitality and longevity.

113
LISTEN—SOMEONE'S TALKING

In my management consulting practice, I'm often hired by a mayor or city manager who is fed up with the planning department. Sometimes, I'm hired by the planning director. Some of these directors are running good programs and simply want to make them better. Others are in trouble, but smart enough to realize they need help.

Of the latter group I've experienced two types. One type listens closely, peppers me with questions, and wants to hear the news, no matter how bad or personal it may be. The other type appears to be listening, but their egos are too big to allow any room for internalizing the issues.

While a few of these directors were eventually fired, many of them reset the direction of their program and solidified their positions. The listeners faired much better than those with their heads in the sand.

During another contract, I was asked to conduct customer focus groups on the permit process for the departments of planning, building, fire, and engineering. At the end of the sessions, I was asked to debrief the department heads. The news was not good. Their first question was, "Have you ever conducted focus groups before?" They proceeded to engage in a childish game of finger pointing.

The focus groups had 60 recommendations that were

implemented. Two years later I was asked to repeat the same focus groups and again debriefed the department heads. This time the news was good. The program had completely turned around, but the key was the new attitude of the directors. No more finger pointing, they had become a team. When told that the focus groups, even though satisfied, came up with another 60 recommendations, they were eager to hear them. They pushed me to make certain I had caught all of the recommendations.

LESSON 113
If we truly listen, we can learn and improve.

114
VENDOR FRIENDS

Theories abound about how private businesses are increasingly finding that having close and cordial relationships with their vendors can add to their bottom line and effectiveness. Most governments haven't discovered this principle. The government approach is often: hire as few consultants as possible, as low bid as possible, and pay slowly or lose invoices.

A few years ago in our firm we created a vendor awards program. We developed an attractive certificate that all our staff signed and several of us would surprise the vendors by showing up in their business for a presentation.

One of our recent clients was a small-to-medium sized midwestern city which had recruited an outstanding young planning director from another state. As an employment condition, he asked for and received a $200,000 per year unspecified consulting budget. This has allowed the planning department to be light on its feet, fill in needed specialty skills, and move ahead. A sensible approach to vendors.

LESSON 114
Make a vendor friend today.

Paul Zucker; Robyn Kettering, Insurance Agent;
Warren Coalson, Zucker Systems

Paul Zucker with Advanced Blueprint manager and
employees

115
CRAB GRASS

During a brief stint as a consultant between my jobs in Fresno and Tucson, I was hired by the University of California campuses at Berkeley and Los Angeles to commission several papers on the topic of growth management and fiscal impact statements and to prepare a paper myself on growth management and planning. These papers were presented at full-day seminars at the University of California campuses at Berkeley, Los Angeles, and San Diego. My paper, prepared in 1974, began by quoting a *House and Home* magazine article that suggested, "The controlled growth movement is spreading across the county like crab grass across the suburban lawn."

The premise of my paper was that you could fly almost any topic you like under the flag of growth management—it's a catchy phrase. When the recession of the early '80s and early '90s hit many parts of the country, the phrase disappeared. In California, Pete Wilson ran for governor with several proposals for growth management, but after the election and coterminous with the recession, the words were banished. Now, as the national economy has heated up, we begin to hear these words again along with its current reincarnation "Smart Growth."

LESSON 115

Keep the words "growth management" in your bag of tricks. Pull them out periodically when the time is right.

116
RAISE MY PERMIT FEES—PLEASE

When I was a planning director, I used a number of consultants, but never for processing entitlements or permits. I felt these were so tied into local policy making and politics that they couldn't be done by consultants. However, I went through the following sequence of events with a client city.

1. We were asked to complete an EIR for a proposed hotel.

2. This led to several other environmental reports.

3. One of the city planners left and we were asked to process a few permits.

4. We were gradually asked to process more and more permits.

5. Another planner left and we were asked to process all the permits.

We charged all the applicants our full-cost recovery fees, which were often higher than the city's normal application fees. However, the developers didn't complain. Why? They received timely, straight answers and processes. Since then we've seen numerous cities use consultants to process planning permits and I've become convinced that it is a viable option for some communities.

LESSON 116
Contract planning is a viable option for the planning permit process.

117
PLANNERS ARISE

One of my favorite cartoons is a planner on his knees being questioned at the Pearly Gates. God says, "Planner of the Week for 1968. That's it?" Not by a long shot. We planners have so much more to offer. But we need to open up, reach out, experiment, change, and challenge.

I hope in this book you've seen that:

- Planning isn't linear.

- You can have fun doing it.

- You can get fired or shot down and live for another day.

- You can learn from dumb mistakes.

What an exciting time to be alive and be a planner approaching the next millennium. If you look up my AICP number you'll suggest it's time for me to retire. Retire? I'm having too much fun. I'm really only getting started.

LESSON 117
Write your own lessons, then write a book.

INDEX

A

agriculture 92-93, 177
America the Beautiful Fund 92
American Civil Liberties Union 111
American Institute of Certified Planners (AICP) 204
American Planning Association 48, 189
annexation 145
Arlington, Virginia 62
Association of Environmental Professionals (AEP) 193

B

Bacon, Ed 9, 20, 180
Bergamasco, Attilio A. 16, 18n,
Berkeley, California 120
Boston, Massachusetts xiv, 51, 61, 180
Boxer, Barbara 111
Brookline, Massachusetts xiii, xiv, 38, (Part 4, 39-63), 69
Brookline Town Meeting 44, 56-57
Bucks County Courthouse 14-15
Bucks County, Pennsylvania 4, 5, (Part 2, 8-21)

C

California Assembly Transportation and Commerce Committee 98
California County Planning Directors Association 178
California Environmental Quality Act (CEQA) 193
California Field Poll 109, 111
California Polytechnic State University, San Luis Obispo 27n
Carversville, Pennsylvania 13
Castle, Louise M. 53
Center for Labor Research and Education 113
Chalfont, Pennsylvania 13

Chandigarh, India 26
charette 32
Chavez, Cesar 113, 119
city and county attorneys 40
Cleveland General Plan 41
Coalson, Warren 201
community development 115-140
Community Renewal Program (CRP) 58
Connybear, Daryl 77
Connybear, Leaf 77n
constituency building 102-103
consulting (Part 10, 187-204)
continuing planning education 107
Cornell University 29n
cost recovery 175
Cranston, Alan 122
Cylinder, Dick 17, 19

D

Dallas, Texas 68, 189
Davis, Bill 19
day care 184
Dotson, Karen 156
Dukakis, Michael xiii-xvi, 44-45, 51
Duluth, Minnesota 4
Dyckman, J.W. (Jack) 25

E

earthquakes 95
economics of development 37
Eichler, Mervin 73
engineers and planners 166-167

F

Fairless Hills, Pennsylvania 16
Fallsington, Pennsylvania 13
Farming on the Edge 92
fire departments 50
firing staff 174
fixed fees 175
focus groups 198-199
Ford Foundation 122

Tucson Comprehensive Plan
149, 150
Twiss, Robert 92

U

University of California at Los
Angeles (UCLA) 202
University of California at
Berkeley 20, (Part 3, 23-38), 107,
140, 202
University of Nebraska 3
University of North Carolina 20
University of Pennsylvania 20
Urban Development Action
Grant (UDAG) 32
Urban General Plan, The 25n
Urban Land Institute 150
U.S. Steel 16-17

V

vendors 200
Ventura County, California 178
Vial, Don 113
Von Gundell, Werner 77

W

Warner, Arlene 61
Washington, D.C. (Part 5, 65-70)
Webber, Melvin M. 25
Weber, Adna F. 29-31
West Side Planning Group 119,
124, 128
Wharton School (Philadelphia)
20
Wilson, Pete 202
Wood, Franklin 9, 17, 18, 19
Wright, Frank Lloyd 67, 88-89,
94
Wycomb, Pennsylvania 12

Y

Yarish, Tom 78
Yield Point Theory 90